Voices in My Head:

Firsthand Account of
Messages From God

The Truth about Angels, Aliens,
Entities, and Ghosts

*I then asked, "What message would you have
me tell them?"*
"Tell them God is real. Angels are real."

Susan K. Edwards

Licensed Spiritual Healer-Coach, Reiki Master,
Certified Ho'oponopono Teacher, Advanced
Pranic Healing®, Lightworker, Sound Healer,
Christian Minister, Psychic Medium, Empath,
Author, Facilitator, and Public Speaker

Voices in My Head:

Firsthand Account of Messages From God

Published by

Susan K. Edwards, dba

Wildhair Studios, LLC

Books that Entertain, Enlighten and Empower

Paducah, KY 42001

© 2020 by Susan K. Edwards

ISBN: 9798554381119

Dedication

I give thanks to the Universe (God), the angels, light beings, spiritual teachers, and all those who lit the path, showing the way. This book is a gift from the angels and your higher self to remind you who you are and to encourage you to return to the frequency of unconditional God Love and joy.

I dedicate this book to my husband, whose unwavering love allowed me to flourish and grow. To my family and friends who stand with me—and continue to love me! To all my clients, readers, and supporters. I thank you from the bottom of my heart.

Contents

Foreword

My statement of faith and belief:

I believe I am a spiritual being having a physical experience. In my pure light form, I am one with the Universe (God). When I am incarnate in my physical form, I am most at peace when I vibrate at, or close to, the frequency of unconditional God Love, or joy. When I am not at, or close to, that frequency, I experience lower human emotions and conditions, like "dis-ease," fear, and anger. The counsel of light beings has sent me (as well as others) to this time and place to remind and teach those who have forgotten who they are and the frequency of unconditional God Love.

—Susan Kae Edwards

The Metaphysician

met·a·phy·si·cian /ˌmedəfəˈziSH(ə)n/
noun: an expert in or student of the
branch of philosophy that deals with the
first principles of things, including
abstract concepts such as being and
knowing.

—Google Dictionary

I've been interested in the metaphysical
nature of my existence since early childhood. I'm
descended from a line of accountants, engineers,
and scientists, and by nature I look at things and
wonder what makes them tick. I've always had a
skeptical eye and will work to debunk or disprove
a theory before I accept it for truth. Even then, I
am willing to adjust my thinking or make a new
decision in the face of new evidence. Which is
good, since a lot of the unseen world is, well—
pretty weird!

Even at a young age, I knew things. I felt
things. I heard things. I saw things in a wildly
different way from those around me. I felt
powerful, even as a young child, but when I
looked around me, everyone else seemed to be
hiding their power, not using it and sometimes
afraid of it. I got the impression that using one's
power, or even acknowledging it, was somehow
bad. And I didn't want to be bad! Like so many

reading this book, I grew up thinking I was the odd man out. I wasn't like everyone else. And I suspect you've felt some of that too.

Looking back, I realize I repressed a lot of exploration of the metaphysical realm and my spiritual gifts as I grew up. Some was due to religious and cultural pushback from those around me. Some was for not having a teacher to show the way. Mostly it was because of my lack of confidence. No one around me was using their superpowers. How could I? Even if no one scolded me for using them, I could see using them was not endorsed.

I put my interest in the metaphysical aside and complied to the thinking of those around me. This stuff was dangerous and not to be explored. People who got involved with New Age practices were blasphemous, evil, and would likely end up in hell. And you wouldn't want that now, would you? Yikes! Of course not!

At fourteen, during my Presbyterian heyday, most of my social life revolved around church-related friendships and activities. I felt all my friends and family were likely heading off to heaven once they died. I certainly didn't want to be left behind or end up in that "other" place, alone.

I never doubted there was a God and enjoyed attending church. But soon I felt disconnected from the message. I felt they were hiding the juicy stuff, and I wanted more information about the magic behind all this. I wanted what I thought the pastors and church leaders had, a direct line of communication to God and deeper answers.

That's where I started running afoul of the *authorities*, the nebulous *they* that no one can identify. I wanted to have a chat with the big guy, a direct, personal conversation. I had questions. It seemed the church leaders were either clueless, or if they knew something, they weren't sharing it with me. I knew there had to be more. I needed more direct communication, even if I wasn't sure how to facilitate that process. My peers didn't have the answers (and not much desire to find out). I would have to seek elsewhere.

Let me stop right there for a moment and clarify my use of the term *God*. I am aware that term is a ridiculously limited concept of something we cannot possibly understand from our human perspective. My concept of God during my youth and my concept now has radically evolved. It is *not* my intention in this book to tell you what God is or isn't. It's entirely up to you to unfold that answer for yourself. I only share my current perspective. It is flawed and limited. Using any label to identify the infinite is amusing at best. But it is a useful trope for the purpose of communicating concepts.

While we're talking about using the term *God*, I'll be using a variety of phrases to describe God. I will switch between more secular terms like the *field*, *source*, *Universe*, or more personal and nonsecular terms, *God*, *Goddess*, or *the Divine*. Plug in the phrase you prefer. Know that I'm referring to the same source energy. Please don't let my phrasing put a roadblock in your reading this book. I'm sharing my current thinking on the nature of the Divine. You make your own decisions.

So what is my current thinking on the nature of God? Well, that's an interesting question. Lately I am more and more convinced that University of Oxford philosopher and futurist Nick Bostrom may have gotten it right when he advanced the theory that we are all part of a massive simulated, albeit virtual, reality.[1] In 2003, he advanced this idea proposing that members of an advanced civilization with enormous computing power might have decided to create simulations of their ancestors.

Understandably, this theory was met with considerable skepticism and some outright ridicule, but he only formalized what many science fiction writers, dreamers, futurists, and philosophers have suggested for some time now.

Since his controversial theory was put forth, it has been tested by many highly respected scientists and philosophers. Turns out it's not as farfetched as you might think. Mainstream scientists and mathematicians calculating the odds favor that we are indeed living in a virtual reality. Yeah. Let that sink in for a moment. Now that's a paradigm shift!

In his series, *Missing Links*, Gregg Braden covers this concept and makes a compelling case in its favor. He gives some tips and tricks on how to interact with the programming to affect your life. I've used several of his methods and had extraordinary success. So I'm leaning toward yes, we live in a virtual reality. But I tend to see

---

[1]Nick Bostrom, "Are You Living in a Computer Simulation?"

it as a divine being (i.e., God) who created the field, not our ancient ancestors.

There is much written on this theory both supporting and debunking its merit. I invite you to do some research and reach your own conclusions. I'll reference this concept when I start to talk about who (and what) angels may be later in this book. In the meantime, I'll be using the terms I mentioned above.

In My Youth

During my teens in the mid-1960s, I was fascinated with the power of your subconscious mind and how to make things happen with your thinking. One of the strong influences in my spiritual growth was José Silva's book, *The Silva Mind Control Method*. According to him, you could train your brain to reach a state of mental functioning called the alpha state.

In that state, you would be able to access all sorts of superpowers to affect your circumstances not afforded to the untrained. He said it was possible for someone to view distant objects or locations and use that information to solve his or her problems.

All right! Now that's what I was talking about. Finally a glimmer of hope. I perceived finding that book as a sign from the Universe on how to access more information about these superpowers I was exploring.

I practiced Silva's methods and did achieve some success. But I needed more. I thought, "Well, maybe the answer to achieving direct communication was in the Bible." Up to this point, I had only studied a few select verses assigned by the Sunday school class.

Lots of folks found answers in reading "the book." Maybe the obvious answer was I should just simply read the book for myself. Seemed like a good plan.

Off I set to read it cover to cover. Oh my. I had some serious misconceptions about the assignment I had given myself. First, I thought there would be a beginning, middle, and end. Nope. We went skipping around time and places. And those names! Egad. I got stuck. But even though I didn't come close to finishing my task, I came away with some observations.

One thing I noticed were all the stories about angels. They seemed to be everywhere. And not just the poufy, incorporeal type. I'm talking the flesh and blood type, with descriptions of what they wore and having them knock on your door.

Angels were everywhere! Wait, what?! They were real? Well, where did they all go? Seriously, when was the last time the news reported an angelic being showing up—anywhere?

Angels are mentioned in religious texts and ancient origin stories all over the world. There are persistent accounts of angelic experiences throughout diverse cultures that date back to antiquity. There are so many stories told so consistently that even the most ardent skeptic must concede that humankind were being visited by someone (or something) greater than themselves, beings they perceived to be divine in nature and from somewhere other than terrestrial earth. *Something* was happening. There had to be a thread of truth to their existence.

If angels were literally walking around interacting with mankind in the ancient past, chatting them up and delivering messages from God—where did they all go? Did they really pack up and leave? Did they just shut down communication and wipe their hands of us? I think not.

Or did they go at all? Is it possible they are still walking around today, interacting with mankind just like they did in the historical stories? Are they simply using the technologies available to us today? Could they still be showing up unannounced and sharing divine messages? Did we just forget how to interact with them?

I suspect you already know my position on this question. But to be clear, they did *not* pack up and head off-planet, never to be heard from again. How can I be so sure of this? Because they are active in my life. They communicate with me, they make themselves known to me, they deliver messages, and they've asked I share those messages with you.

As you read this book, I will share many of my firsthand stories of encounters with these divine beings. I find they are active and as full of God's messages as ever. Any of their messages will be in italics. I edit those very little to preserve their original intent.

I'll also share stories of others that have had direct encounters with angels. There's nothing special about me or those I document in this book. *You* can also have angels present in your life. You need only make space for them at your table. They are eager to join us. They're simply waiting for your invitation.

The Awakening

Despite not being able to plow through reading the Bible cover to cover, I continued to seek lots of alternative materials exploring metaphysics and spirituality. I met new like-minded people and developed a broader understanding of spirituality. I got bolder in the exploration of my gifts and metaphysics in general. Focusing my energy on that goal provided me with a steady stream of new books, classes, and friends that were stepping-stones in my quest to understand the world and how to use my gifts. The Universe was sending me the answers I sought.

My awakening took off full steam when I finally started trusting my higher self to see *my* path over the limited perspective of the humans in my life. It took me a long time and a lot of self-work to trust that new perspective and find my confidence. We are conditioned to conform, to doubt our own connection and believe we can't possibly be worthy of the attention of angels and God.

There are often societal consequences if we don't conform to rules and regulations. My current spiritual path has cost me more than a few relationships. So I get it. You may not yet be ready to follow your path. But when it *is* time, you will know, and you will have no other choice.

In the meantime, celebrate wherever you are on your personal journey. It's exactly where you need to be. If you've been drawn to this book and these stories, then you are ready to accept the gift from the angels. Are you seeking validation that you are ready? Here it is.

You are ready. You are worthy. You are already in touch with angels. Get quiet and trust what they share with you.

Finding Myself

As I got to know myself better, I learned I am a lightworker, empath, and a psychic medium. More specifically, I'm a light-bringer. I'm here to serve humanity as well as our planet. My mission on planet earth this life cycle is to bring light and remind people who they are and to teach the frequency of unconditional love.

As for my gift of psychic mediumship, I can tap into the universal stream of knowledge or the "field," and I can communicate with nonphysical entities. That includes passed loved ones, and spiritual entities like angels. I don't typically see things with my human eyes. I sense them. I know things. I hear things. Some people will have one or more of these gifts, which are often referred to as clairvoyance, clairaudience, claircognizance, or clairsentience. We'll talk more about the differences later.

An empath is highly sensitive to frequencies, especially the frequencies of other people's emotions. The gift of empathy got me into a lot of trouble growing up! Until I understood how to manage it, my healthy boundaries were pretty much nonexistent. Anyone without healthy boundaries sets themselves up for all sorts of chaos in their life.

Empaths living without heathy boundaries create a breeding ground for unbalanced relationships with family, friends, lovers, and coworkers. They often become magnets for people who feed off other people's energy, aka energy vampires. Unbalanced empaths usually become dumping grounds for all the problems and chaos of people who are happy to take advantage of others while they shirk responsibility for creating balance in their own lives.

Yup. That pretty much sums up the first two-thirds of my life experience.

By now, I'm confident a few of you are seeing yourself in this story. My experience is likely paralleling some of what may be going on in your life as well. You may be feeling chaos and frustration with yourself because you also engage in an endless string of unbalanced relationships and situations that don't work out in your favor. Worse yet, they leave you drained of your energy, joy, and vitality.

I'm happy to report that by the very nature of acknowledging that you've got these gifts, you've taken the first steps to managing them. And managing them is the first step to a more balanced life experience. It doesn't matter whether you choose to use your gifts daily or put them in a shoe box locked in the back of the closet. Managing your gifts will help steer your life and relationships in a much more balanced and pleasing way.

Additionally, it's going to make the space in your life to communicate not with only your higher self but with angels, light beings, and other spiritual entities that are available to help guide you.

Let's face it. If you have "gifts," you've probably known about them since you were a child. I doubt you were invited to talk about them, let alone explore them. Perhaps you were even told those gifts, and by extension, you, were evil, just by acknowledging them.

I'll stay out of that debate in this book other than to say these tools are gifts from God. You were born this way. These gifts, much like a hammer, can be used to create beauty and function or to bash in someone's head. Same hammer, different intent. Be mindful of your intent. Keep it pure and centered in unconditional love, and you will stay out of trouble.

Do you have to have special gifts to be able to connect with angels? No, you do *not* need to be a psychic or a medium to have angels in your life. However, if you do have gifts, your awakening will be more intense.

Keeping My Guardian Angels Busy

I grew up the consummate tomboy, and I often joke that as a child I kept my guardian angels busy. I saw a funny meme the other day. I thought it fit perfectly!

"I'm pretty sure my guardian angel just sits there watching me while painting her nails and rolling her eyes."

You could always find me climbing trees, running, jumping, and doing other generally risky behaviors. So yeah, I'm pretty sure that was written about me!

I recall a winter trip as a tween with my bestie and her family to a nearby state park. She and I were roaring around looking for fun things to do and happened upon a mostly frozen lake. I say mostly because we had to jump over the thin ice close to shore to get to the thicker ice further out. I still remember the sound of the ice crackling beneath our feet. Don't worry, this story has a happy ending. Neither of us had any notion that we might fall through the ice. It never occurred to us as a possibility. And we didn't fall through. I suspect it took more than a few guardian angels on that excursion!

I went to school with this bestie, and our elementary school building was brick with a decorative concrete ledge that flared out a few inches all around the building. The ledge was about four feet above the ground. One day, she and I wondered if we could shimmy our way around the entire building on that ledge. Challenge accepted!

We climbed onto the ledge and, using the space between the bricks, held on with our fingers. All was well until about a third of the way around the building. We happened upon the first stairwell that led to a lower level. The drop was no longer going to be four feet but more like ten. With stairs. I remember looking at her, wondering if she was going to call it. Nope. Well then, neither would I! I remember feeling a bit nervous, not that I would fall, just that I needed to concentrate harder.

Repositioning our fingers in the space between the bricks, we kept scooching our feet along the ledge a few inches at a time. The skin on our fingers took a beating from the rough bricks, but we made it all the way around the building. We were quite proud of ourselves.

Oh, and I can't forget the giant sycamore tree in her yard. We named it Old Faithful. Even then we knew it was more than just a tree. It had a real personality. We never referred to it as "the tree" or "the sycamore." It was always Old Faithful. It was very nurturing. There was this one large branch that swooped down close to the ground, as if to say, "Come on girls, climb on. It'll be fun."

Who were we to refuse such a kind invitation? We would climb high enough to see all the way into the downtown area about two miles away. The branches at the top of the tree were small and tender and groaned under our weight. Happily, neither we nor Old Faithful suffered a single mishap or fall over the years we climbed.

Looking back as an adult, I must have been testing the limits of my physical body in the world in which I had awoken. Obviously, I survived my childhood. Even then I think I was aware of the active presence of angels in my life.

While my body reflected my chronological age, I don't remember ever feeling like a child. I gravitated toward adults and clearly remember high levels of frustration when I pontificated gems of universal wisdom in their presence but was rebuffed as a mindless toddler and adolescent.

I saw reality from a radically different point of view even at the tender age of five or six. I was always observing the goings on of life from a distance. I was often amused, frustrated, and annoyed when those around me just could not see how things worked at the energetic level. Of course, I had no idea of any of these advanced concepts. I just knew their way wasn't the way I thought the world worked.

As a result, early on I was convinced that my entire family was insane. And not just in the figurative sense. Literally! How could they possibly be so stupid as to not see what seemed so obvious to me? Of course, they were not mad hatters. Nor were they stupid. They simply chose a different spiritual path.

I spent a great deal of energy early in my life trying to convince people of my "rightness." I needed them to validate me by agreeing to my point of view. I would happily spend hours in arguments to "help" them see how I was right. You can imagine how much of my time and energy was wrapped up in conflict.

After several decades of personal work, my thoughts on "being right" have evolved. Life is much easier now that I've largely given up the notion of right and wrong. I no longer need others to agree with me to validate my world view. Being right isn't all it's cracked up to be. Whew. What a relief! I now have a great deal more time and energy to pursue my divine assignments.

I tell you this in hopes that it may help you with your situation, whatever it may be. I've always communicated with the higher realms, angels, light beings, God. Talking about that to others usually resulted in serious pushback and sometimes ridicule. Often it resulted in them becoming "very concerned" for me and my soul. After all, they wanted me to fall in line with their worldview and set of rules to ensure I would go to heaven. Their stated motive—which sounds high minded—is that they could then be with me for eternity. That logic amuses me, since some of those so concerned about my final destination choose not to spend much (if any) time with me here on earth in the present. They might want to reconsider their wish to spend eternity with me.

I now recognize their real concern wasn't so much that I won't make it to heaven but that *they* won't make it to heaven. Think about it. If *my* worldview is right, that must mean *they've* got it wrong. I suspect their true desire is that I validate *them* in their understanding of how to behave and think here on earth. It's always very threatening to face a possibility that you got it so wrong.

Here's the thing. They don't have it wrong. Neither do I. We just picked different majors at the Earth School University. And like any university, you get to select your courses and time needed to complete the course of study and your payment plan. You get to choose when and how you learn the curriculum. Understanding this gives you latitude in creating harmonious relationships with those who see the world from a different perspective.

So Are You a Lightworker?

If you are drawn to this book you, too, are likely an outlier with gifts that others don't possess or haven't acknowledged. You may be a lightworker, empath, psychic, medium, or a mixture of all of the above.

You may have suspected it for some time, but it doesn't match up with what your friends and family are experiencing. That can leave you feeling like an outcast, a weirdo, and more than a little bit crazy.

You're not crazy.

But neither are they. You are simply on a different spiritual path and are awakening to the job you agreed to before you showed up in this particular "skin suit" in this particular lifetime.

So what is a lightworker?

Here's how I've come to understand what that means. A lightworker is a soul, a being, or an entity that is striving for, or has achieved, the frequency of divine, unconditional love. This being is dedicated to holding the space for light and love. Lightworkers show the way through their actions, words, and message.

You are drawn to these messages because you crave validation that you are sane, rational, and on your soul's correct path. My wish for you is the gift I was given a few years ago by the angels: the gift of validation that you are not alone. That the voices in your head are light-bringers, whispering divine messages in your ear. That you *are* a lightworker doing your soul's work. The Divine is active in your life (even if you're not yet aware), and you are the master of your experience.

Many of my encounters and messages were channeled through meditation and written down so I would remember and recount them accurately. My intention is to stay true to the core message.

It is also important to note that when communicating with the Divine, angels, or higher spiritual beings, they don't speak in English. They typically use images and emotions or light languages (aka speaking in tongues.) At least that's how they communicate with me. When I share their message, I will use terms that are from my personal life experience. They show me the image or symbol, and then I do my absolute best to translate it into a message that makes sense. Depending on your gifts, you may hear, see, or feel the message in an entirely different way.

You're Not Crazy

I was in my twenties in the 1970s and attended a Unity church in our area. Unity could be considered a "new thought Christian" denomination. From their website, Unity describes itself as "a worldwide organization offering an approach to Christianity which teaches a positive approach to life, seeking to accept the good in all people and events." It was founded by Charles and Myrtle Fillmore in the late 1890s in Kansas City, MO.

I had grown up in the Presbyterian denomination but found myself veering off their more mainstream doctrines. When I met the Reverend Bette DeTurk at the new Unity church in my area, I resonated with her and the Unity message. I stayed with that church for many years and learned many important teachings.

I remember coming home from a particularly moving church service on one of those perfect summer nights in the 1970s. My husband at the time and I drove up to our modest house, and he went directly inside. As I got out of the car, I lingered and looked up into the clear, star-lit night sky. The temperature hovered around seventy-five degrees. The air was crisp without a drop of humidity. I was physically comfortable, and emotionally I was still buzzing from the message.

I continued to think about being connected to the universe and all that is in it. A wave of gratitude and absolute knowing washed over me. I began to cry, not with sadness but out of joy and gratitude. I was one with all of creation. At that moment, I was connected. I can still feel that joy of knowing and that sense of belonging. I also knew I had a divine assignment, even if I wasn't clear what it was or ready to take responsibility for it. But at least, in that moment, I had tuned in and clearly heard their message.

My next validation that I was a spiritual being having a physical experience came with my first out-of-body experience somewhere in the mid-1970s. I practiced yoga with my friend Pat.

She helped me explore the more esoteric aspects of life and how I apply them in my own life. When Pat suggested I try astral travel and out-of-body experiences, I was fascinated. Always up for an adventure, I wanted to try it.

I achieved my first successful "trip" during one of Pat's yoga meditations. Our group met in the party house of the apartment complex where I lived. Like many apartment complexes, one of the amenities was a common building that could be used by residents for their sanctioned gatherings. Yoga was trending at the time, so the complex manager granted us permission to use it for class as long as anyone in the complex could attend.

The room itself was like most party rooms: spacious, with neutral decor, and well kept. The wall facing the complex's pool was lined with several sliding glass doors, which provided lots of natural light in the room. There was a large area in the center with carpet, with some tables, chairs, and sofas easily pushed out of the way to make room for our mats. A small area on one side had a kitchenette and area for food prep and serving. The room had a high, vaulted ceiling with decorative wooden beams.

During class that day, I got into a lotus sitting position, and we began our group meditation. After a few moments, I was aware of my physical body directly below me as I hovered high on the ceiling. I remember thinking, "Wow, this is so cool!" Then I remember thinking, "Oh…I'm really up high," and whoosh! That sensation of fear sucked me right back into my physical body. It would be years before I was able to have my next out-of-body experience. But being able to experience that validated that my higher self, soul, or whatever you want to call it, was indeed independent of my physical body.

In the 1980s I was having more success controlling my out-of-body experiences. I could have remote meetings with people when it wasn't possible to meet in person. I tested the accuracy of the experience by picking something in the room they were in and commenting on it. I wasn't always accurate, but I was often enough to know my skill was improving.

My angelic connections were also increasing, but I was still trying to walk with one foot in the three-dimensional world and one in the spiritual dimension, not committing to either. That schizophrenic approach left me spinning my wheels. I wasn't completely successful in either world. My relationships were not healthy. I was not healthy. My career was lackluster. I was allowing myself to get distracted from my divine work.

I overconsumed everything—food, sex, alcohol. Anything to numb myself to the reality that I would have to make a choice or continue to live in a constantly chaotic state. Fear of facing the consequences of my decision kept me straddling the fence.

During this period of time in my life, I flirted with making the commitment to a spiritual lifestyle. I did some psychic readings for friends and family. I was in demand due to my accuracy and people's innate need to be validated. Unfortunately, spirit made it clear that I was *not* allowed to charge money for the readings. I could accept love offerings, but they put the prohibition on going professional. That made it tough to create a stable income. I wondered at the time why I was not allowed to charge for readings. But I never had any doubt they weren't negotiable on the subject.

I now realize that the prohibition was in place for my protection. It takes maturity and experience to be able to spiritually counsel your client with no regard to compensation. It freed me from feeling the need to construct a story designed to please the client in order to be paid and have them return for more of my services.

To this day spirit suggests I not charge for the information, as it isn't mine to sell. I am, however, allowed to charge for my time and experience. I've spent hundreds of hours and thousands of dollars perfecting my skills through workshops, certifications, retreats, and education. My time and experience are valuable, so there is no longer that prohibition imposed on my spiritual teaching and coaching.

During that time frame in the '80s, I gave a few metaphysical seminars and workshops. I also considered buying a metaphysical bookstore. I was fascinated with the subject and felt at home there. I didn't get too far into the process. I mentioned it to those close to me and was met with extreme disapproval from some.

At that time I was nowhere close to having confidence in myself, my gifts, or my spiritual path. I wasn't able to weather their harsh judgment and disappointment directed at my plan. I buckled to the pushback and walked away from the opportunity. Once again, I conformed to other people's expectations for how I should live my life.

In the 3D world, I started new businesses and relationships. I tried to manifest more than a mediocre income. Neither my spiritual nor 3D endeavors were very successful. I wasn't willing to commit to one path or the other and accept the consequences for making a decision. I was afraid to claim my truth. I hadn't found my voice or the strength to take a stand.

In the '90s I met and married my current husband. I had grown up enough to be ready and able to exist in a stable, healthy relationship. It took me three tries, but we are about to celebrate our silver anniversary! He is the perfect match for me. Our marriage and love for one another has offered me the emotional stability I needed to finally settle down and face my fears about myself and my spiritual path.

He's a nonpracticing Catholic, so I still had some cultural and religious pushback. But his unconditional love and the foundation of our marriage allowed me to confidently move into the spiritual river of my awakening. He still thinks most of this stuff is, as he puts it, "weird," but he has had enough firsthand experiences through all this that even he acknowledges something is going on.

Since 2010 my awakening has taken center stage. I guess it's about time. After almost seven decades on planet earth, it was crunch time.

One of the major turning points was a trip to Arkansas for a crystal dig. On the advice of a friend, I went by myself. That trip put an end to any of my ambivalence. It was amazing to connect with Mother Earth. Sitting in the dirt digging for her crystals, I felt a vibration. At the time I wasn't sure what I was feeling. I now know it was the frequency of the crystals. I was finding some crystal treasures, but toward the end of the day of digging, I was led to move to one final dig spot.

I started poking around in the dirt and soon pulled out a spectacular quartz crystal point. As I rubbed away some of the mud, I could see more of the crystal, and I began weeping. It felt like I had just reunited with an old friend. This was *my* crystal. It was a Lemurian seed crystal, and as I rubbed it, I activated a soul-level lesson.

For those not familiar with crystals, I'm sure this sounds more than a bit odd. Crystal hounds get it. Trust me. When you connect with a crystal, it's real, and you know it at the center of your being. I connected with this crystal.

The folklore on Lemurian seed crystals says before the ancient advanced race of Lemurians left planet earth, they "seeded" their knowledge base in certain crystals. You can tell a Lemurian crystal by examining the sides. If there are what looks like barcodes in the structure, it is a Lemurian. If you rub those barcodes, and you are ready, you will activate a life lesson. These crystals are somewhat rare and always make their way into the hands of whomever is ready for that lesson. It's quite magical.

Apparently, I was ready. As you might imagine, this set off a series of wild, intense, life-changing events.

I had become a Reiki I practitioner back in the '70s. After a short time, I allowed the chaos swirling around distract me and I let my energy work go dormant. It would be a forty-something year delay before I revisited Reiki. Within a few short years of finding my crystal, I became a Reiki master. I learned vibrational sound healing. I studied frequencies and how to utilize them for healing. I explored my psychic and mediumship abilities. I started purposefully connecting with the angelic realm. I became a licensed spiritual healer-coach. I got certified in Ho'oponopono, which is the ancient Hawaiian practice of reconciliation and forgiveness. I opened a rock shop and metaphysical resource center, all in the middle of the Bible Belt, no less!

In other words I stepped into my soul's true path. I accepted the consequences for making my decision. I was no longer confused. God was calling me to get my act together and get about my soul's work. I accepted the job. And it felt amazing!

Don't get me wrong. Not everyone suddenly got on board with my new direction. Quite the opposite. I lost some relationships along the way. Some were significant, but I was OK with that. I made my decision. It was suddenly abundantly clear to me. I could listen to humans and fear-based thinking, or I could listen to higher sources, God, the Divine, angels, and take their advice. It was my choice.

I still get things wrong sometimes. I am still studying to perfect my connection to the Divine. I still get pushback. But after all the direct validation from the spiritual realm and the angels, I am confident of my path. I know if I step off it, I will be guided back to the highest path.

In relating how long it took me to step up, it is my hope that you stop being so hard on yourself. This stuff isn't easy. It runs contrary to mainstream teachings. It's often hard to step out on faith when you feel alone or different. Give yourself some grace. You are exactly where you need to be. When you are ready, you will take the next step on your path. Or not. You get to choose.

We want to provide spiritual comfort and a deep, deep knowing you are never alone. A warm, divine hug anytime you need it.

—Archangel Raphael

Validations

People often go to psychics to get validation on something they already know or at least suspect is true. We all want to be sure we are making the correct assessment of the situation. I'm no different. Especially in the beginning of my journey.

I started seeking validation that I was indeed in touch with the angelic realm. As soon as I looked, I found it everywhere.

Here is one of their messages to illustrate that direct communication. I had been doing a lot of one-on-one healings with clients at the Rock Shop (my store), and it was great. Many of the healings were physical. Some were spiritual, some emotional, and some were soul level. Several might be considered miracles. But there was a nagging sense I was missing something, that I was to be doing more.

I think we are all victims of thinking too small. We couldn't possibly be as powerful as we suspect, could we? It's difficult to believe we have unfathomable power to shape our reality. I still struggle with the depth of possibilities some days.

This message came the first time I hosted the holy archangels in my home. I've put the information on how you can host them yourself at the end of the book. During mediation on June 14, 2016, I used "automatic writing," one of my methods of channeling divine messages. I've also created a YouTube video on this message from Archangel Michael. His message was regarding self-doubt and the impact that one or a few can have on the greater good. Here was his message to me.

> *We are well pleased that you are touching and influencing as many people as possible. To awaken the masses. It's fine to work one-on-one, and that is important. But we grow impatient in your reluctance to claim your full power and responsibility. It's time to fly. Off the wire, chickie-poo.*

The wire analogy is from one of my favorite riddles. "Three birds are sitting on a wire, and one decides to fly away. How many are left?" The answer is three. Just because a bird *decides* to fly away doesn't mean he actually did it. It was a direct message, in a language that I would understand, to get off my butt!

> *You are to help millions, not just a few. Get on with it. We have demonstrated that we are here and with you. We will assist you in your job. Literally and every way possible. You have said you agree to be a human interface. So let's get going! Time is passing*

quickly. You have much work to do. It's time to get on it. Desperate people are desperate for the message of hope and love. Evil has their ear. And it is loud and persuasive. We must not allow its message to be the only message.

I then asked, "What message would you have me tell them?"

Tell them God is real. Angels are real. We grow impatient with lip service, and now we want people to take responsibility for their lives. To hear the truth. Not just the lies of evil. You are all children of the most loving God. Which makes you family. God has made no mistakes.

You each have a lesson to learn here on earth this incarnation. Stop trying to force your lesson on others. That's their lesson. Stop listening to false prophets. Your very survival [mankind] depends upon it.

The time has come for all to know the truth. Those who are unprepared will not fare well. We have no choice but to amplify the vibrations toward the love frequency and do it fast. Evil has become aware it might lose and has amplified its efforts to keep mankind and indeed planet earth in the lower frequencies. It is their food. Nourishment after all. It will not give up easily or quickly.

"So what is our first step?"

Stop listening to the lies. Turn off the media after you get the basics. The rest is mostly opinion and conjecture. Go out. Touch people. See for yourself. Of the billions on this planet, only a minor handful of people have changed the mindset and lowered the vibration of so many to that of fear and loathing for each other.

Technology, it is great and terrible at the same time and has made that possible.

You can see how a relatively few can affect a great number of people and alter the course of mankind. You have that proof. That is your proof each of you can also have the same impact. But that of love. We desperately need peace warriors right now. Wage love with your heavenly brothers and sisters. Wage love with each

other. Do it! Do it now! Before it
is too late, and this beautiful
planet and all mankind is lost. Do
it now.

That was an intense experience. I could feel the urgency in his message, but who am I to affect millions? I didn't know how to do that! But I accepted that with the help of the Divine, that's exactly what I would do.

Then came the message, from June 15, 2016.

> *We are helping you as we*
> *have always helped you. We are*
> *pleased that you are no longer*
> *afraid and stepping up into your*
> *job. Finally! We will help you*
> *help mankind in this age of*
> *technology. To use it to reach*
> *millions. We are pleased you are*
> *open to us coming. You are*
> *powerful, and we will nurture you*
> *to fulfill your full potential. We*
> *will be here to help you.*
> *—Archangel Michael*

With that validation my confidence soared, and I fully embraced my assignment, knowing the angels had my back.

Who and What Are Angels?

Let's step back for a moment and discuss who and what angels are. I'll begin by stating I am *not* an expert on angels, religious literature, or the history of cultures. This is simply *my* understanding of angels at this point. That understanding is evolving. I'm learning. That said, here's my understanding up to now.

In 2016, I was privileged to attend an angel seminar taught by the international teacher Master Nona Castro. Master Castro was a personal student of Grand Master Choa Kok Sui (MCKS) and a senior instructor for Higher Pranic Healing courses worldwide. She also lovingly served as a mother superior in a Catholic convent in the Philippines. She is considered an expert on angels. I learned much about the nature of angels from her.

According to her teachings and the teachings of others, we come into this world with at least two guardian angels. They are assigned to guide and protect us as we move through our life.

While our two assigned angels stay with us throughout our life, we can always access other angels by asking for their help. But there's a catch. You must ask for help. They will not intervene without your invitation.

Due to the nature of earth being a freewill zone, intervening without your express request would be an infringement upon your free will.

That's the key point: angels *must* be invoked. In every channeled message I've received from the angels, they constantly reiterate the need for us to ask for help. I've sensed a bit of frustration on their part that more people are not reaching out to them.

According to most historians who write about this subject, angels are selfless servants of God. They often come to deliver God's messages, help us, guide us, and protect us. Within the angelic realm, there is a hierarchy. Angels are happy to serve, in part because they evolve through their service.

As selfless servants they have appeared to mankind throughout history delivering God's messages. The word *angel* can be traced back to the ancient Greek word *angelos*, which translates as *messenger*.

According to the Google dictionary, the definition of an angel is "a spiritual being believed to act as an attendant, agent, or messenger of God, conventionally represented in human form with wings and a long robe."

As my concept of God evolves, I find my thinking of the nature of angels has also evolved to include ascended masters and other light beings.

I'm not sure angels were "created" by God or if they are evolved entities that are resonating close to the frequency of unconditional love, and we perceive them as divine. I also accept they may simply be interdimensional beings or advanced, enlightened extraterrestrials. Like I said, I'm still exploring my understanding of them.

A far more radical concept is that angels are actually "nonplayer characters," or NPCs. If we are indeed experiencing a virtual reality as I spoke of earlier, then this explanation makes sense.

It could explain their ability to be everywhere and anywhere, seemingly at the same time. It also explains why they must be asked for help and for their devotion to helping us navigate this life experience. They are designed to help and guide us. I don't know! I'm still processing that possibility. But what I can be sure of are my personal, firsthand experiences.

How to Connect Personally With Angels

I may not be able to tell you exactly what they are, but I can tell you my personal experience with angels and angelic beings.

It's intense!

I think most of us become aware, at some level, when we are in the presence of angels. I have several common experiences when they are close.

First, whether I'm in a dream or altered state such as meditation, I experience intense bright light. I can't look at them directly. It hurts my eyes. The light is so intense I can't make out any specific shapes. Just a brilliant ball of light. Even if I'm in my dream state, I still can't look directly into the brilliant light.

Next, I feel their energy. The atmosphere around me changes. It is more charged—like electricity. I'm aware of their presence. I may see them in my mind's eye. Their energy is as intense as their brilliance. I may start to get what I call an energy headache. My physical head doesn't hurt. It's the area around my head, my aura, my crown and third eye chakras, that gets uncomfortable.

I almost always get emotional. Not being the emotional type, this was a little weird for me at first. I couldn't figure out why I was all choked up with emotion until I recognized it as the emotion of gratitude. Now I use my tears of gratitude as the barometer of where my emotions lie and the presence of these divine beings. These higher emotions can signal you are about to connect with the angelic realm.

I am also emotional because I feel their unconditional love. Being in the presence of the Divine is like coming home. You breathe a deep sigh and know you are deeply loved and accepted. It's an amazing sensation. That's how I know angels are around.

I will sometimes experience more discomfort in my physical body. That happens if I've not been careful about my nutrition or emotions. Also, if I'm stressed out or hung over from fear, stress, or other physical excesses, I feel more discomfort.

We are, by our very nature as humans, dense energy. We must be to move around in our 3D world. On the other hand, our souls are pure spirit and resonate at a much higher frequency. To experience life on earth, we must inhabit terrestrial bodies. Only then can we touch, taste and experience physical life.

Making Space for Angels in Your Life

What does it mean to make space for angels? Think of the spiritual nature of an angel. It is considerably higher in frequency than our physical bodies and lower emotions.

Sometimes our denser bodies are not be ready to handle the significantly higher voltage of these divine beings. Imagine a high-voltage light plugged into an old-style cord that is designed for a much lower voltage. If the wire is not designed to handle that higher load, pumping all that extra voltage through it might heat up the wire and sometimes blow a fuse!

I'm not saying having angels around will blow up your fuse box! Nope. What I am saying is if you have a clear intention to work with angels on a regular basis, you will need to be mindful of having a "wire" that is built to handle the higher voltage.

How do you do that? Well, replace any of your old "wiring." Get rid of old ways of thinking, behaviors, or habits that create wear and tear on your physical and energetic bodies. Lifestyle choices that age your body make it hard for you to connect to these higher frequencies. If your physical body is clogged up with poor nutrition, stress, gunk from your daily thinking and being, then you've got a pretty sludgy mess for that electricity to try to run through.

Clean up your act. Eat mindfully. Learn how to be conscious of your thoughts. Learn to pray and meditate. Give up your addiction to negative thinking and emotions. Limit self-destructive lifestyles and toxic relationships. Fall in love with yourself and with life. Upgrade your frequencies closer to joy and gratitude. Consciously make space for angels and higher beings.

Through several of my channeled sessions, the angels have explained connecting to them this way.

As an example, imagine an old-style radio with a tuning dial. If you wish to listen to a particular station and the musical playlist it offers, you must first plug your radio into a power source—source energy—and turn it on. Next, you must be tuned into the station's frequency to receive your desired broadcast station.

You can do this through meditation, prayer, or elevated emotions. Let's say you decide to listen to pop music. If your local pop music station's call numbers are 101.5 FM, in order to listen you would need to tune your dial to 101.5 on the FM spectrum. If you have used this type of radio, then you know that, when you get close, the station starts to come in. The closer you get the "sweet spot" of 101.5, the clearer the station becomes, and you can listen to the playlist of pop music.

The same can be said of connecting with the angels and the spiritual realm. If you wish to make the space for angels to work with you in a more consistent, powerful way, you must tune to the frequency of their radio station.

There are many ways to accomplish this. Here are a few that I've used with success.

First, you must learn what station they are broadcasting on. If you wish to connect and communicate with angels, you can be certain they will not be found down in the lower emotions of fear, anger, frustration, jealousy, greed, self-loathing, or resentment.

To tune to their station, use your emotions. That's right. Thoughts, feelings, and emotions all have a frequency to them. To raise your physical or spiritual frequency, you need only raise your emotions. Joy and gratitude are great emotions to strive toward. You can get closer to those higher frequencies deliberately, even in the midst of personal turmoil, but it takes some practice.

Connecting to the Angelic Radio Station

Of course, the tried and true ways of meditation and prayer should be the foundation of any work you do when reaching out to the spiritual realm. It is only when you learn to control and quiet your thinking brain that your higher self and the angelic realm can clearly be heard.

I can hear you now regarding meditation. "Oh, I'd love to meditate, but I can't. I can't sit still long enough. I have tried, but I just can't!" Sound familiar? Or how about this? "Yeah, I know, everybody tells me I should meditate, but my mind's racing all the time." Well, folks, if that's what is happening—you need to meditate!

I remind people they *can* meditate. I tell them I can prove it. It's then they look at me like, "Yeah, right. OK, whatever, Susan." Here's the simple exercise to prove you can meditate.

Follow these instructions. For the next few seconds, I want you to close your eyes and observe your thoughts. It doesn't matter what you're thinking; just observe your thoughts. You ready? Go!

OK, were you able to observe that you had thoughts, or did you observe, "I had no thoughts"? The question is: who was doing the observing? Ah, good question, huh? Yes, the answer is your higher self. That's your superconscious, the real you.

If you were able to observe your thoughts (or lack thereof), then that is concrete proof that you are not your thoughts. You are the observer of your thoughts.

Wow! That revelation can be life altering. Think about that for just a minute. Often we believe our body *is* our mind. Many believe we are our thoughts and that our human chatter-brain is what's running the show.

This little exercise demonstrates that you are *not* your thoughts. They are merely thoughts. Thoughts are the stories we tell about ourselves and our world. Some of these stories aren't even our stories. They're stories others told about us, and we ended up believing them. Parents, siblings, relatives, and friends all contribute.

A lot of people are tortured by negative self-talk: "I'm not worthy, I'm too big, I'm too small, I'm too stupid, I'm too smart, I'm too…" whatever. Those are just your thoughts, stories—they are not you. The true you is your soul, your higher self. That's who was doing the observing in that little exercise I had you perform.

If you were able to observe that you are separate from your thoughts, that's the first step to being able to learn how to meditate. And that, my friends, is life altering. If you're having a life that you're not particularly thrilled with, meditation is a tool that can radically improve and change your life. You can improve your life by simply controlling your thoughts.

Is that always easy? Well, not always, especially in the beginning. Think of it this way. Do you have or have been around an unruly two-year-old? Think of your brain like that unruly toddler, who is whatever your age is—twenty, thirty, fifty years old. If you haven't disciplined your two-year-old toddler brain for fifty years, and all of a sudden you say, "Listen, I want you to sit down in this chair and be quiet for the next twenty or thirty minutes," what do you think your toddler brain is going to say?

"I don't think so!" Followed by a full-blown hissy-fit.

And why would it cooperate? It's gotten its way running the show for this long, and like with any unruly toddler, to effect change, you have to be consistent. You have to be gentle. You must be firm and have fair guidelines. So how do you go about this? Well, the first thing is to acknowledge that you are not your thinking. Your thinking is just your thought-stories.

There are countless articles and innumerable medical studies that have shown meditation is good for your mental and physical health. It improves your peace of mind and your happiness.

When your body is in a constant state of stress from a real or perceived threat, it diverts all its energy to survival. Fight or flight. That's hardwired into all living beings. In this state, the body determines that it's not safe to take any energy and turn toward repair work, growth, or relaxation. Those are optional if the physical body isn't going to survive the external threat.

If your body isn't taking time for repair, you are setting it up for all manner of physical and mental wear and tear. Learning how to control that unruly two-year-old toddler and training your body to get into the present moment— however you manage that—isn't just a good idea. It's critical for your best health.

If you want to connect with angels, then you must learn the technique to dial into their station.

Learning how to raise your vibrations, tuning into their frequencies, is fast and easy when you learn to quiet your mind. And meditation is a great tool.

Raising Your Frequencies in a Hurry

If you've learned how to quiet your mind—great. But sometimes you need to raise your frequencies in a hurry, and there's no time for a meditation. Here are some other methods I've found helpful.

Clapping while singing happy upbeat songs is amazingly effective in bringing your frequencies up quickly. It feels very silly at first, but keep it up! Laughing, even a fake laugh, will work. Do it long enough—say thirty seconds or so—and you likely will begin laughing in earnest. Reach for the emotion of gratitude. Bounce your body. Almost anything that gets your heartbeat up and you feeling happy works well. Puppy and baby kisses are givens!

Monitor your internal chatter. If it's negative, clean it up. That negative self-talk is nothing more than false narratives others have told you about yourself. It's simply an old, stale story you continue to repeat. The reason it feels so bad is because you know those stories don't reflect your true nature. You *know* it's not your truth, and your higher self refuses to agree with you and go along with the BS.

If you've had a lifetime of others telling you these falsehoods, it will likely take some concerted effort on your part to make the change. First, you'll need to accept it's false and then to rewire your brain to reflect your truth. Meditation will help with this issue. If you've been acting out to validate their low expectations of you, you may have some "cleanup on aisle nine" you need to do.

Don't despair. It will only take as long as you want (or need) it to take to get into the flow of life, love, and positivity. You are *not* doomed. You are meant to live a life that is filled with joy and abundance. After all, you are a child of God. You are literally made of the same stuff as the stars. This is a rich and abundant universe. You have an inheritance that is waiting for you to claim. You need only accept your good to receive the blessing of a joyful existence. You are, after all, the architect of your life.

"That's just great. But my life is a mess."

The nature of a crisis leaves you no time to consider anything but your priorities. That is the gift a crisis gives you. You get to review what is working and what is out of balance in your life.

Get quiet and go within. What is disrupting your life? What's disrupting your lifestyle, your comfort, your joy? Reflect upon that.
Pay attention to what false narratives you may be giving power to that are causing this imbalance.

Fear is a big one. Fear is a separation—a disconnect from

unconditional love. Fear is not real.
Fear is an illusion you are giving power
to. —Archangel Ariel

Write the stories you tell in your journal. What are some of the false narratives you are giving power to right now? Ask yourself, "Whose stories are these?"

Chances are these are stories you either heard early in your life by parents, siblings, or friends, or you constructed a story to explain something you couldn't understand at that age in your life. They likely have nothing whatsoever to do with you. Instead, they are constructs of an immature mind trying to make sense of dysfunction and chaos around it.

We come into this world without preconceived thought, emotions, or attitudes. We learn all that from the people and environment around us.

If dysfunctional people surrounded you early on, chances are the stories about yourself are dysfunctional.

Often fear sits smack in the middle of these false narratives.

Fear: you are unworthy. Fear: you don't fit in with others. Fear: you aren't lovable. And it hurts, even though they are falsehoods.

How to Fix It

One way is to call on your angels for help. As you learn how to make space for angels in your life, call on them for help. They want to help. They are here to help. But remember, you must ask for that help.

If you chose a life lesson that creates destruction in your life, family, or even the world, they are there if you want to switch stations and tune into a different, happier life lesson. Remember in the radio example that the angelic station is constantly broadcasting and available to you anytime. But you must turn on the radio and tune into 101.5 FM to receive it. They will never force you to tune to a particular station. That's not what they do.

What Can the Angels Help You With?

Along those same lines, I sometimes get questions about what you can request of angels. One example was a friend that was not experiencing joy from our current political administration. She asked if the angels could remove the president and put in someone that was aligned with her worldview.

I suspect you already know the answer to that question! Uh, no. That's not in their job description. The angels do not take sides or have political preferences. Back to the freewill zone issue. Rich life lessons can be learned from every choice we make, individually and collectively.

After I had a couple of prayer requests and questions about what you can ask angels to "do," here is what the angels told me about their role. Their answer is clear.

We don't tell the human population what to do.
—Archangel Michael

God presented us with free will, and it's up to us to decide what it is we do with our life and which lessons we choose to work on this lifetime. With that understanding, you can see angels would never tell you what to do.

What angels *can* do is help you get clear. They can help you rid your life of the illusions and the clutter that might be clouding your judgments or impeding your decisions. They can help get your soul's energy and frequencies lined up with the frequency of unconditional love.

Once you get the clutter out of the way, and you've tuned into your true soul-self, the answer to your dilemma will become clear. You will know your best course of action. It's not up to angels (or anyone else, for that matter) to tell you what to do. That would be an infringement on free will, and that's not the angels' role.

Can I Ask the Angels to Make Me Rich?

If wealth is what you are looking for, the angels are not going to help you by providing the winning lottery numbers. Nope. Not going to happen. Ask instead for a prosperity mentality, and know that this is a rich and abundant universe and there is plenty for all! Tune into the feeling that you are worthy of being prosperous.

Here are the instructions channeled in July 2020:

> *If peace is what you desire*
> *Live peacefully moment to*
> *moment*
> *If love is what you desire,*

Let love temper all you say,
do, and feel
If prosperity is what you
desire,
Live in abundance
If health is what you desire,
Live sustainably.
—Archangel Michael

As humans, we manifest things. We make stuff. We make cars and TVs and radios and computers and tables and chairs. We take ideas like, "I need a table to eat my dinner on," and we bring it into the 3D world. That's one of the things we humans do.

If you're tuned into the Divine, and your heart is pure, and your intentions are clear, you can manifest all sorts of wonderful things in your life. Health, happiness, joy, harmony, prosperity for yourself and your family and lots of people around you.

If you're not tuned in to that frequency and your energy is spent arguing and complaining and saying ugly things about everybody and everything, then manifesting wealth will not come easy. It can be done, but the way in which it comes into your life may be less than divine. Generally, you will attract whatever you focus on into your life.

That makes it truly critical that we as individuals and as humankind start tuning into a much higher frequency. With the advent of all the social media, we have the ability to connect with people literally all over the world, nearly instantaneously. If we all dial to the station of joy and happiness, that's what we're going to get.

If we all dial to the illusions of separation, chaos, dissonance, anger, and war, that's what will show up more frequently.

A critical message from the archangels was to get clear about your true intentions. Get clear what you want in your life, and get clear about what's coming out of your mouth, what activities you are spending your energy doing and supporting. Make sure that if you like jazz, you tune into the jazz station.

This is a channeled message from Archangel Michael in June 2017:

> *Be clear about what you*
> *desire and focus upon it*
> *with unwavering faith.*
> —the Archangels

How to Address the Angels

One thing I want to make a note of is that when I speak of the angels or call them in for help, I always say, "Holy Archangels" or "Archangels." They've made it known to me that I'm not on a first name basis with them. So I don't call them and say, "Hey Michael, how ya doin'?" It's "Holy Archangel Michael." These are messengers of the Divine. And when you ask for help, do it with humility and respect. Be specific in your request, and leave it open for that or something better. Finally, thank the angel(s) for their assistance.

Asking the Right Way

If you are looking for a lover, asking an angel to deliver your true love will likely convince you they are not real and don't answer your prayers. You should already know by now that's not how they work. Instead, do your work. Learn to love yourself. Fix what isn't working in your current relationships. Ask for help with that task. Then you will be tuned into the angelic station and be able to receive true love when it shows up in your life.

And please don't bother asking an angel for something that is designed to manipulate or harm someone, nature, or the planet. Never ask for something to happen to others. Yikes! If what you are asking for isn't lined up with God's divine laws and the highest good for you and for all, they are not able to respond.

If an "angel" does show up and offers to do your bidding, beware! They are *not* from the highest source for your highest good! Not all "angels" are divine.

How to Ask for Help

Let's take the example of a prayer for healing. This was a prayer request from a woman named Sonia.

"My friend's niece was born prematurely this morning. Can you ask the angels to help?"

I suggested they reach out to Archangel Raphael, as he is one of the healing angels. I instructed them to get quiet, and in their prayers for their friend's niece, say, "Holy Archangel Raphael, please come and help in whatever way that would be appropriate in this healing. I let it go to God and to the Archangels. I bless and thank all the physicians, the attendants, and everyone who is to be involved in this healing. I ask that, whatever man can't do, the healing hand of the Divine steps in and completes the healing. I ask for and know that this healing is complete at whatever level is most needed and proper. Thank you, Archangel Raphael, for your help."

I then suggested she breathe and know that the angels are with her and they are there to help.

Using the broad terms such as healing at whatever level is needed and most appropriate allows the angels to work for the highest good. Remember: earth is a freewill zone. From our point of view, it is often impossible to know what lesson a soul has selected for this lifetime. Not all healing takes place at the physical level.

It's difficult to imagine that our ardent prayers for healing go unheeded and our loved one experiences a death of their physical body. Many a person has had a crisis of faith at those difficult times. It's important to remember the part of us that never dies is our eternal soul or spiritual self. Our eternal soul must reside in this physical body for us to experience physical life on earth.

When the physical body perishes—and they all do—death does not touch the soul. Sometimes healing is meant to take place at the spiritual level. When we ask for healing at whatever level is needed, we leave it open to the best and highest level of healing available.

Does is suck when someone we care about and desperately want to stay alive leaves us physically? Yup. It hurts. We grieve. We miss them. We're angry. These are all normal and healthy expressions of emotions during great loss. Grief is natural. But when we are clear that the eternal soul has not died, simply separated from the body, it becomes easier to move through grief back into joy.

How Do I Know If This Is a Divine Being?

I said earlier that my experience with angels is bright light, intense energy, and an overwhelming sense of gratitude and humility. I can tell I'm in the presence of a higher being.

If you encounter an entity that is "not of the light," so to speak, you will most likely not feel overwhelmed. Their energy is so much lower and a frequency that is closer to ours, and therefore we are more used to it.

They may present themselves to you in a way that is confusing. Perhaps they are pleasing in appearance or take on the form of a person or animal you trust. They might promise you any number of things you desire. They may offer you something, in return for a small "favor" from you. Hang up that phone! This is *not* an angel from the highest source.

Think about this for a moment. If the entity you are communicating with is truly from God, what could you possibly offer them? Seriously. Only lower entities need something from you. And trust me, the cost of these favors is high. You can look through history to see the chaos they've wrought in many lives over the millennia.

Angels from the highest source will never agree to help you manipulate or harm anything. Use your discernment when communicating with the spirit realm.

What Happens at Death?

I've asked the angels about this on several occasions. Here's how they've explained physical death to me.

> *Your soul, or the spiritual part of your being, your higher self, is pure spirit. It resonates at a much higher frequency. It is what animates your body. This is your connection to God. It is the spark of life that animates all living things.*
> —Archangel Azrael

All things, including the physical body, have a frequency. The body functions best around sixty to eighty hertz. That's thought to be the sweet spot. If our frequency gets too low, our bodies start getting uncomfortable. Colds, disease, and all kinds of malfunctions can happen.

If you've ever been in the presence of a corpse, it is clear that whatever animated that body or that person isn't there anymore. It's like, "Where did it go?" There are many theories of what happens upon death. Here's what the angels told me:

Your body and its frequency
are dense because you're walking
around in a three-dimensional
world. But your spirit is a very
high frequency. It must find some
common ground where your high-
frequency spirit can reside with
this low-frequency physical body.
—Archangel Azrael

This sweet spot, or common denominator, is how you exist in the 3D world. The body's frequencies can go lower if we don't take care of ourselves physically. Sometimes trauma happens, you're under constant stress, or your lifestyle causes issues. When that happens, there is less and less space where the high-frequency spirit can co-reside and animate the physical body. That common denominator space gets thinner and thinner when the frequency gets too low within the physical body.

We've all known people and thought, "I don't even know how that person is still alive." That's what we call the will to live. It's when our higher self, or our soul, decides to lower its frequencies to continue to animate the physical body. Maybe the person doesn't feel like their soul work is done, or they still have something they must learn or do before departing. The person stays alive, even if it's at a very low level. Somehow life hangs on.

At some point your higher
frequency soul can't lower its

*frequencies any further. Doing so
ceases to be advantageous. At
that point, the soul doesn't have a
common denominator frequency
in the physical body in which it
can reside. When that happens, it
cuts its links with the physical
body. That's what you call death.
It's the separation of the spirit
from the physical body.*
—Archangel Azrael

Sometimes, for a variety of reasons, the spirit can reestablish a connection with that physical body, and we say, "They came back from death." It can happen, but you still have to have this common-denominator frequency.

For example, someone has a heart attack and dies on the operating table. The doctors get out their defibrillator, and bam! They bring the frequencies of the physical body back up to a place where there is a common frequency where the soul can live. The soul can then reanimate the physical body, and then life can go on.

Sometimes when there's been a trauma like an accident or murder, the spirit is abruptly separated, and the soul is left in a traumatic death state. In some cases, the soul can get stuck. This is what we call ghosts or spirits, and sometimes they do need help to pass on.

Past-Life Commitments

Take the story of a woman who had recently suffered a miscarriage. She came to the store to gather some crystals and incense for a burning bowl ceremony and memorial for her son. I offered condolences but could see that, while she was grieving, she knew something more was happening.

With her permission, I tapped into the soul she had miscarried to see if there was any communication about why he had chosen to not fully manifest into her life.

It was clear they had very deep soul ties. They had shared a past lifetime as close friends who went to war together. He had died on the battlefield and not been properly buried. As the surviving friend, (s)he committed to righting that situation at some point, burying him with honors and helping his soul pass over into the light. His purpose showing up in her life so briefly was to fulfill that soul-level contract.

When I shared that with her, of course the tears flowed. But beyond the sorrow of not spending a life together, she felt relieved to have confirmation of what she already knew. The purpose of his passing was to honor that commitment. It all made sense to her now.

I saw her again about a year later, and she shared the joyful news that she was pregnant again! She had no fears of losing this child and told me the ceremony had been so healing. It was the perfect way to say farewell and celebrate his life. She understood why things unfolded the way they had. She had buried her friend with honors, and both of their souls were at peace.

The Long Road Home

In the 1990s I had a lot of pain in my right foot due to a bone spur and scar tissue resulting from an earlier surgery. Thirty years and forty extra pounds didn't help, either. I was facing another surgery when I met a man who offered to do some energy work to see if he could help. I was familiar with Reiki, but he insisted that wasn't his method. I didn't understand exactly what he was talking about, but, always curious, I agreed.

We sat down opposite one another, and I removed my right shoe. He put my foot on his knee and took a deep breath. He began to move his hand around my foot without touching it. After a few moments I could really feel energy swirling around my foot from his actions.

The energy in my foot had been stagnant for so long; it felt a little like when a body part falls asleep, and the pins and needles as it wakes up and energy starts to flow again.

I was fascinated. I wanted to know how he was doing this, and how I could learn. He gave me the name of the woman and her book, which I found and bought. Honestly, I don't remember her name or technique now. I tried what she suggested but wasn't able to replicate the experience. I set it aside and figured it was another mystery I wasn't able to crack. Turns out it just wasn't my time, and I wasn't ready to accept those esoteric skills yet.

Fast forward about a decade, and my interest in energy work was reawakened after the crystal dig I talked about earlier.

I also started pursuing other energy workshops. I studied frequency and sound healing with a brilliant woman, Dr. Christi Bonds-Garrett. She is an MD, acupuncturist, and teacher. She's the founder of AromaSounds and creator of harmonic techniques incorporating tuning forks, gemstones, color, light, and essential oils known as Harmonic Touch Therapy. She's an expert in Chinese healing— among many other things—and has written numerous books. I was lucky enough take several classes on her Raindrop Harmonics techniques.

During her workshop I met so many interesting people from all over the world but struck up a lasting friendship with Sabrina. She is one of those interesting souls that has traveled the world and, indeed, the universe, both physically and energetically. She is a shaman, yoga teacher, psychic, medium, and energy worker. She's amazing, and when I need to really understand the energetic side of things, she's my trusted go-to. Clearly, we were longtime soul-buddies and delighted to have rediscovered each other this lifetime.

I had recently dug my personal crystal and mentioned it to her. She suggested I bring it to class the next day, which I did. During a break she offered to connect with it and channel whatever she discovered. I had been very protective about letting anyone touch my crystal (that's another crystal thing), but I knew it was OK for her to handle it.

She held the crystal in her left hand and held my hand with her right and tapped into the energy. Ho, boy! That was a wild ride! She immediately began speaking in light language, and I felt a bolt of energy like that from a live wire coursing through my body. I felt amazing, excited, energized, and confident. For no obvious reason, I began crying.

This continued for a few moments. When she finally stopped the download, we just stared at each other. After a moment, we both burst out in laughter. It was like two kids just getting off the most exciting roller coaster ride. We were exhilarated, and I was amazed. This was nothing particularly new for her, but for me—it was definitely a new experience.

If you're not familiar with light language, here's how Yvonne Perry explains it in an article, "What Is Light Language?"[2]

"Light is information that contains the codes of creation. Geometry is the foundational structure for art, science, music, and architecture. Its images, codes, and shapes are found in DNA, crystals, atoms, mandalas, hieroglyphs, and pyramids. The language of light is a sacred geometry produced by vibration. Light Language is a powerful sacred gift that gives purposeful expression of love from Creator."

Perry says it is similar to speaking in tongues, and that it is the language of the soul. I don't

---

[2] https://weare1inspirit.com/what-is-light-language

understand it at a conscious level, but somehow, I understood what Sabrina was saying at the soul level.

Sabrina said there was an entity in the crystal. Her name was unpronounceable, but we could use the nickname Ohmrah. Ohmrah was with me in Lemuria and was thrilled to be uncovered and reunited. But there was a deep sadness in her, which may have been a part of why I was crying. I wasn't sad. It was more like I felt Ohmrah's deep sorrow. There was also joy to Ohmrah's energy, joy that she was back and could be of use. She longed to be useful.

No worries there! I have been engaging with her ever since. When I need serious, "big dog" crystal energy, I bring her out. Her sadness has completely dissipated, and she and I continue to work together.

It became clear during that session at the workshop that I was getting the first of several large downloads.

OK. Spoiler alert. If you think this stuff happening to me is all a bit "weird," hang onto your butts. This train was about to take me places that I fully admit seem…well, crazy. That's the thing about having an awakening. When you truly surrender to your soul's mission, you must be willing to step beyond the known, to step outside of your comfort zone and accept there is *way* more to this than we think or have been told. So buckle up, buttercup! Get prepared for this story of my awakening to get weirder and more wonderful.

Of course, everyone's awakening will be different. I can only tell you how mine is unfolding.

Back to the workshop. Sabrina then asked me very nonchalantly, "So did you feel that download?"

"Uh, well, I felt something…" I had felt a definite surge of energy into my body, but I had no idea of its significance.

"Yeah, they were doing some DNA downloads." Her casual nature in delivering this information led me to think I might have missed a memo somewhere.

"Oh." I tried not to seem too oblivious to that which she might be referring. Who were the "they" in this context? And exactly what were they doing to my DNA? I felt like the neophyte who stepped into a high-level class late in the semester when everyone else had a firm grasp of the material. It seems like you should understand, but you are clueless as to what the heck they are talking about.

She could tell I didn't comprehend what she was telling me and patiently started explaining.

It's important to know I've never once doubted the existence of extraterrestrials, angels, spirits, or ghosts. I'm a fan of the science fiction around these subjects, read about it, talk about it, and I'm comfortable around these issues. But there comes a time when it's no longer folklore and it's presented as fact. It's a strange moment when they are no longer stories but related as fact by people who have considerably more experience than you. Now it's an entirely different ballgame. But there I was. Batter up!

Sabrina patiently explained that the "they" to which she referred were benevolent ETs that were working with me in my awakening.

OK, time out. Aliens have been working with me? To upgrade my latent DNA to my full potential?

"Yes, they were downloading some necessary codes to reconnect and upgrade your DNA. This will allow you to reach your full potential in your role as lightworker."

Sidestep here. There are volumes of information written about our so-called junk DNA. Many think it is actually DNA that connected us to these different realities in the ancient past. Some say overlords purposefully "unzipped" or disconnected it to keep humankind in bondage and under control. I'll not get into a lot of that detail in this book, but I would invite and encourage you to do some research on this subject to learn more.

The break ended, and it was time to resume the workshop. We returned to our seats, but I was eager to have dinner later and hear more about all this!

By the end of the day, I had time to process a little of this. We met for dinner, and I had a barrage of questions. Who were these ETs? What role did my crystal Ohmrah play in all this? What was all that light language earlier? Was I going to sprout antenna? Yikes! Was I going crazy?

Good news. No antenna. ETs were benevolent. Finding Ohmrah was a trigger. I had volunteered for this. Whew.

Wait. What? I had volunteered for what? I wasn't aware I had signed up for anything.

It was time for me to come face-to-face with my lifetime of denial.

Denial that I was different. Denial that I didn't have a larger…in fact a *much* larger purpose during this lifetime. All my life I had been unwilling to acknowledge my true path. This was one of those pivotal moments. I had to choose between the "red pill" and have the unpleasant truth revealed, or the "blue pill" and remain in blissful ignorance. (Watch the 1999 movie *The Matrix* for context.)

I did not hesitate. I chose the red pill.

The servers that night must have wondered what we were talking about for the next few hours. She took me on a wild ride through the cosmos, different dimensions, worlds filled with wonder and dangers. She opened my eyes to a much richer reality.

I'm sure the past few pages may have some of you rolling your eyes and putting this book down because it makes you uncomfortable. That's OK. But what if, for just a moment, you suspend what you *think* you know and follow me down this rabbit hole. Certainly make your own decision when you finish this book, but I challenge you to read on. Take a look at your own life. If you are exceedingly uncomfortable with the next few chapters, could it be because you know it might apply to you too?

Again, quoting from the 1999 movie *The Matrix*, Morpheus warns Neo, "Remember, all I'm offering is the truth. Nothing more." This is *my* truth. Yours will be different.

The Red Pill

Part of the inconvenient truth I learned that day was that my DNA is a human-alien hybrid and that my higher soul-self agreed to come to earth. I gave permission to reconnect my DNA to better accomplish my mission. I answer to a Council of Lightbeings which consists of any number of sentient beings, including angels, ETs, Fae and interdimensional entities among others interested in preserving earth.

(I did warn you this was about to take a left turn into uncharted waters.)

Deep breath. Go refresh your beverage, use the potty, and settle back in for the next part. It's about to get good. Much has been written about humans having hybrid DNA. There's lots of ancient and current folklore about aliens coming to earth. some benevolent, some not so much. Seems they were all doing some manner of genetic manipulation on the indigenous species of earth. I'll not be covering that subject here, merely accepting it as a basis of my experience. There is much solid literature on this subject. I invite you to do your own research.

Over the years since then, it has been revealed that my DNA tribe is that of the Mantis race. I know this ET race has gotten some pretty bad press, especially around abduction stories and association with the Grays. There are also good things they have brought to mankind. They are often associated with healing, arts, science, technology, and knowledge. All I know is that I and the beings I work with are working to the benefit of Earth and all her lifeforms.

At this point, you may be wondering if this is still a book about angels. Yes! It is. But let's face it. It's a slippery slope if you give angels credibility for being real. If they're a reality, how far left of that point of reference is the existence of any number of other noncorporeal or non-terrestrial entities? I warned you, that pesky red pill is inconvenient.

It's safe to say this information took a minute for me to process. One of the more hilarious fun facts of my life is that one of my great-great-something uncles on my maternal side of the family is the French naturalist and entomologist Jean-Henri Casimir Fabre. He lived in the late 1800s and was a prolific author known for his lively style of writing. He wrote many popular books on the lives of insects and is still known as the father of modern entomology. Yeah. That's the branch of zoology concerned with the study of insects.

I know. The irony isn't wasted on me.

Since that first time, I've received numerous additional downloads, some to upgrade my DNA, some informational, and some physical. It's important to note I am asked for, and I give, permission before these downloads happen.

If you think you've been a victim of unauthorized alien abductions, downloads, or implants, that is a different situation. There is help, so don't despair. But I'm not covering that in this book, because that's *not* what happened to me.

Coming to Terms with Uncomfortable Truths

As you might imagine, this new narrative didn't match up to any of the stories I believed about myself. I decided to do a past-life regression with a certified hypnotist to explore some of these possibilities.

The session revealed several lifetimes that involved alien encounters. Interestingly, my personal folklore never included any ET stories. My previous past-life stories centered around life in Old England, Wales, and that area. One of those lives included being burned for being a witch. I even have a noticeable speech impediment that sounds a lot like a British accent. I spent a year in speech class at age seven trying to learn how to say *r*. But no ETs popped up in any of my stories.

During the past-life hypnosis, two lives involving ET encounters stood out. One involved me in the jungle many thousands of years ago. I was hunting monkeys and heard something off in the distance. I quietly made my way to the ruckus and observed a landing craft and many aliens around it. I watched for quite a while, undetected, before hurrying back to my village.

I gathered several of the men in the village to accompany me back to the spot where we all were able to observe the aliens as they packed up and left.

I became an important elder in the tribe and was known for my animated retelling of the story to many generations.

Hmmm. Wonder if that's where I learned how to tell stories?!

The other lifetime recounted during the session that involved ETs was one from ancient Egypt. I was number two to the Pharaoh. I was again a man in this lifetime and was attending him as he lay dying in his bed.

I recalled the elegant palace and surroundings. He was in the final stages of life, and I was extremely sad. We were close, and he was beloved. I was younger than he. I may have been his son. When he passed, a spaceship arrived to take his body. I helped load him onto the ship.

The crew asked if I chose to stay on earth and assume the role of Pharaoh, since I was next in line, or leave with them. I said to them, "I want to go home," and left with the ship. I don't recall where "home" was.

In a later chapter, I will talk about a third lifetime memory I recovered, which explains the memory of being burned as a witch. I've never been consciously aware of any of those memories. But there they were.

Soon after the hypnosis session, I attended a light language workshop with Yvonne Perry. Attending the workshop was a profound experience for a number of reasons, not the least of which was that I came face-to-face with my Mantis tribe. I've never been aware of speaking in tongues or any other light languages. After the experience with Sabrina, I wanted to explore this intergalactic possibility. While I didn't think I spoke in tongues, all my life I had used a series of whistles and clicks to connect with critters and birds. I'm an avid birdwatcher, and so it's not unusual to hear me vocalizing to communicate with them. Turns out that *was* me speaking in a light language. Who knew!? Since that workshop, I have spoken in light language only a handful of times. I never know when it will pop up, but I don't repress it. I let it rip and simply trust my soul has something to say!

During the early part of the workshop, the attendees were seated in a circle, facing toward the center. The instructions included becoming aware of the two assigned beings directly behind each of us and to begin talking to one another and the beings in the circle in light language.

We were to let go and practice feeling comfortable yakkin' it up. Yeah, I wasn't really feeling it. I tried a few times, but I let my human inhibitions limit my participation. Most everyone else was really getting into it, and there was a palpable buzz going on in the room. I was very aware of my two attendants, but they, like I, seemed impatient with all this chatter.

I remember looking over to a gentleman seated across the circle from me who was also mostly silent. We didn't know each other but instantly connected telepathically. We looked at one another and started a private, silent conversation. Our attendants were quite irritated with all this mindless chatter. They were ready to get the meeting started. It seemed they had agreed to attend because of the gathering of all these star seeds and other galactic participants.

We were both aware of their arms crossed and tapping their feet in impatience.

Without a single word spoken, we both knew exactly what was being said and began laughing at the impatience of our companions. It was like the boss waiting for everyone to settle down and get the meeting started. I asked him about the encounter later in the day, and he confirmed that's exactly what he was experiencing also.

During the meditation portion of the workshop, we were invited to connect to our intergalactic family. I must say, I wasn't really expecting much, but as I meditated, I experienced this large Mantis entity in front of me. I was somewhat startled but took a deep breath and relaxed back into the experience.

I compare it to finally facing your deepest fears about yourself and coming to terms with the issue. It was OK. I wasn't under threat, and we were connected in the deepest way possible.

We also had a segment where everyone was to write in light language. I began to doodle, but it felt contrived. I regathered myself and began again. This time I did a single symbol and then, below it, wrote the translation. This felt quite natural, and so I continued that the duration of the exercise. Naturally, I was the only one who didn't write a story or poem. Seems I was a translator!

That actually makes some sense to me. I have always been someone who takes complex information and translates it into more comprehensible bites to teach.

New Chapters Begin

By now, the Rock Shop had many wonderful people and opportunities coming my way. The store was doing well, and my skills were unfolding. Still, it's a challenge to accept some of what your awakening brings your way.

If you felt separated from most of your friends and family before, trust me—you ain't seen nothing yet! And can you blame them? This stuff is so far off the collective narrative, it stretches anyone's ability to believe it is true.

This is where the rubber meets the road. You must decide. What *do* you believe about yourself and the very nature of your existence?

Are you a physical being having a spiritual experience or a spiritual being having a physical experience? Those are really different approaches. If you are merely a human trying to understand the meaning of your life and not extend that questioning to the spiritual nature of your existence, then I suspect you've had a frustrating life trying to make sense of your gifts. Things don't add up when you limit your possibilities to what they taught you in kindergarten.

It's not until you cross through the veil into unlimited possibilities that you can really start to see the true nature of your existence.

Should you accept everything and anything you see or read? I hope not! Now, that would be crazy!

Nearly every human in your life will try to talk you off the ledge. They will become exceedingly uncomfortable as you move further away from their worldview. They will likely quote whatever spiritual tradition you grew up in as evidence you are wrong and going to wind up in hell. You may lose some relationships. You might lose your job. Only you can decide if that is OK. In the long run, choosing this path is the easier choice. But like all choices, there are consequences.

Divine Assignments

By this point in my journey, I no longer have any doubts about the spirit realm and my commitment to be a lightworker. It's real. I'm all in.

The first location for my rock shop was in the 200 block of Broadway in historic downtown Paducah, Kentucky. It was all of about four hundred square feet, and two blocks up from the confluence of the Ohio and Tennessee Rivers in an old building. I went small since I wasn't sure I could make a living selling rocks. I certainly wasn't sure they wanted a metaphysical shop in the heart of the Bible Belt. Turns out my fears were for naught. Business was brisk, and when my lease was up at the end of the year, I moved to a much larger space in the 300 block.

During my first year, I got to meet the ghost in the building in the 200 block. My ghost buddy kept breaking the locks and hinges on my doors. After about three rounds of this, I was getting frustrated.

The last straw came when I had a woman in a wheelchair with her companion in the store. It was a few hours before a parade was to take place. The pair shopped for a bit, paid for their purchase, and went to leave. We could not get the outside front door open. It was completely jammed.

Once I realized I wasn't going to get the door to budge, I made a quick call to the building maintenance man. He got there quickly and tried to open it from the outside. He also couldn't get it to budge. Happily, the two women in the store took it all in stride after I explained my theory of what was happening.

Finally, he removed the outside hinges, removed the glass door, and the ladies were set free! I compensated them with some choice crystals and a future store credit for their patience. I think they enjoyed having a story to tell.

That was it. I had a little "meeting" with my ghost buddy and asked what his issue was! Seems he had been the owner of the shop during the '50s and '60s, and he was very unhappy with the current owner's remodeling.

He used to put his granddaughters in the front windows, where they could watch the downtown parades. The new barrier walls meant there was no line of sight to the front windows from the back of the shop. He expressed his displeasure by breaking the locks on the doors blocking his view.

Once I understood the issue, we agreed to compromise. I pledged to leave the door open anytime there was something of interest happening on Broadway. In exchange, he would leave my doors and locks alone. That solved his issue, and we no longer had any door or lock issues.

He wasn't really the problem.

Old buildings with lots of history and river energy can sometimes whip up other, baser entities. You guessed it. Something much darker also lurked in the building. This was not a ghost but something much older and decidedly not human. There was not much I could do to get rid of it completely, so I committed to keeping the frequencies in the store at a level that would keep it at bay.

I cleared the store when I arrived in the morning and cleared it before I left in the evening. It worked, but it took constant maintenance.

Just when you think it can't get much weirder—yup. It got much weirder. In the fall of 2014, a few months after I opened the store, I got a visit from Amy Allen, a medium who is one of the hosts on the popular paranormal show *The Dead Files* on the Travel Channel.

She introduced herself and told me she was working on an episode regarding a property about thirty minutes away in the neighboring community of Mayfield, Kentucky. I was the only metaphysical shop in the region, and she needed some supplies. She also said she would be referring the family to come in for items to clear the property. I didn't think too much more about the meeting. It wasn't until much later that I would learn the significance of that encounter.

Soon enough, the property owner, Socorro, came in with a shopping list. She was a lovely woman, but I could tell she was extremely stressed. We chatted while I filled her order. There was no one else in the store, so I asked her to fill me in on her situation. I am a fan of paranormal ghost hunter shows. Naturally, I was curious. She told me some of the details. It was not good. Her problems included the usual noises, electrical issues, things moving, doors opening and shutting. Much more troubling were the violent attacks on her and her husband. She was being punched, and he had been tripped and had fallen down the stairs. The family's overall health was being affected. Their two daughters, eight and fourteen, were both under attack and terrified. The problems weren't contained to the house. There were also serious issues with the land. I would soon find out just how dangerous the land was.

Research on the property showed it had been a successful tobacco farm for at least 100 years. Oddly, during the last 130 years, that property had forty-seven turnovers. One person kept the property only ten days!

On September 2, 1939, seven farm workers on the property had been out cutting tobacco. As they headed back to the barn to hang it, a storm blew up, and lightning struck all seven of the men. They all went down. Four of them died.

Over the next few months, Socorro made numerous trips into the store for crystals, incense, supplies and advice to help her in the quest to clear her property and protect her family. We got to know each other as she would update me on the latest medium or shaman that would come to help her family and clear the situation at the property. Much work had been done, and things had improved. Among the protection methods I had suggested was my protection bracelet. I outfitted the entire family with them.

These are simple bracelets I create with obsidian, amethyst, and rose quartz beads. The beads are strung on a waxed cotton cord. It's adjustable in order for you to wear on your wrist or ankle. I program them to be diversionary crystals, meaning if you are under psychic or energetic attack, the bracelet attracts the energy and diverts it safely away from you, grounding it in Mother Earth. The obsidian also forms a shield of protection around you, reflecting negativity. The amethyst protects you from psychic attack, and the rose quartz helps keep your heart chakra protected but open to love. The bracelet is designed to be worn twenty-four seven and can be expected to last at least six months before the cord wears out.

If the bracelet breaks significantly before that, it's a sign it's doing its job and has "taken the hit" for you. We offer one free replacement if that happens within the first thirty days. If the crystal breaks—yikes! You really need to put up your energetic shields. You are under attack!

I tell you about these bracelets because I've lost count on how many this family has gone through. I'll talk more about this later, but hang onto that thought for now.

Things would get better for the family and then relapse. Socorro was increasingly desperate for relief.

One of the findings from the show was Socorro herself was unconsciously inviting evil in through her anxiety and negative thinking. I coached her on some ways to become more positive and did a lot of energy and soul healing. I provided a lot of vibrational tune-ups to help during her visits.

During a vibrational tune-up, I use a 432 hertz tuning fork and chime around the client's aura, or biofield. This clears stale energy and releases stress. It autotunes and balances their chakras. I cut soul cords and ties, and close any rips, tears, or holes in their aura. In a matter of a few moments, clients report feeling lighter and considerably better emotionally.

The work of the shamans, mediums, and healers had rid the family of most of the issues from the ghosts that were taunting them in the house itself. The property, however, still had lots of problems.

There's a big difference between pesky ghosts and poltergeists, shadow people, evil entities, elementals, or demons. Ghosts and earthbound spirits are, for the most part, something you can deal with. Smudging and general cleanup of the energetic environment will often do the trick in clearing them. Usually a medium, shaman, or medicine man can help spirits who are stuck in their death state or who are merely looking for help to cross over. Dealing with the other entities is dangerous and not for the uneducated.

Evil Dies Hard

Things were better but nowhere close to being safe. She asked me again for my help. Nothing else was working, and she didn't know where else to turn. She was convinced I was the one who could help. I wasn't so sure.

I was completely unqualified and told her so. Remember, this was still early in my awakening. Exorcism was decidedly *not* my wheelhouse. Nope. Sorry. Got the wrong gal. Wish I could help. Best of luck.

Then I got the assignment. The angels told me to go. Ho, boy!

I don't know if you've ever tried to argue with angels, but I find it's pretty much a waste of time. I really didn't want to do this. I had no experience in anything more than smudging and blessing my home and property. This was way over my paygrade. Not to mention I was scared! I don't do dark, scary stuff well.

My angels and guides assured me they would be with me. I finally surrendered and set up a time to go out to do an assessment. No promises! Just an assessment. We agreed on a Sunday afternoon. I took my husband, Robert, with me, and we set off to take a look.

As we drove up to the property, I felt a sense of dread. It was hard to know if it was my anxiety or if I was feeling something from the property. I reached into my pocket to reassure myself that my crystal, Ohmrah, was there and immediately put up my energetic defenses. I reinforced the energy bubble around myself, my husband, and the car. I took a deep breath and tried to relax.

The house was on about two acres of land located in a rural subdivision. There were neighboring houses, but they were spread out. The homes in the area were roomy, and the exteriors were well kept. Clearly this was a prosperous area.

Socorro's property was located on a corner lot, and we turned onto the side street and pulled into their driveway. A white fence surrounded the grounds, which sloped slightly toward the center of the property. There in the center of the land stood their large, modern two-story home. It had an attached garage and a detached outbuilding. There were a few trees scattered throughout the lot. The grass was mowed, and the landscape around the house was neat and well kept.

Pretty average-looking large house on a roomy lot. OK. Not too scary.

We greeted Socorro, and I met her husband, Tim, and their two young daughters, Bianca, fourteen, and McKenzie, eight.

Pleasantries aside, she brought me inside to walk through the house. It was a warm, sunny day, and Robert branched off and started walking around the property outside.

He claimed he was only along for the ride and to help me if I needed him. Secretly, I think he was just as interested to see if this place was really haunted. He, too, has denied his spiritual gifts all his life. He's a sensitive and a medium.

He sees things with his human eyes. I "see" things with my third eye, or psychically. However, when confronted with the evidence of his gifts, he greets it with snorts and guffaws of denial. Nope. Not him. He's just there to help me. Uh-huh. Sure…

I knew I was being watched inside the house, but whatever or whoever it was knew enough to keep a distance. Plus, the family had already had numerous healers, mediums, and shamans come do work on the home. Socorro and the family also smudged nearly every day and used incense to keep the space clear. They had employed several my recommendations, and they had done a good job. I sensed a few hot spots, but the house felt livable. I made some notes and headed outside.

When I met up with Robert, he reported he had felt something following him the entire way around the property. He was slightly creeped out but brushed it off as his imagination. It wasn't.

The property had a decidedly different feel to it than the inside of the house. It was obvious the efforts of clearing by the family were focused on their living space, not the property. Things felt much more unsettled and threatening outside.

Behind the house they had a sizable aboveground pool with a wooden deck around it. That area creeped me out and felt the most active. The entire time I spent outside, I didn't see a single bird or squirrel in the trees. They would sit on the perimeter fence, but they didn't enter the property. Socorro confirmed in the five years they had lived there, not once had they observed birds or squirrels in the yard or trees.

Oh boy. That's not a good sign!

As I walked around the property, I found several vortexes and portals. They were powerful and felt extremely chaotic and dangerous. Socorro told me the others had pointed out the portals and explained what all had been done so far. No one had been able to close the portals, despite attempts to do so. Whoever (or whatever) created them clearly didn't want their doorways closed and created them to be unstable.

The land also had a lot of underground water veins, which all met up in the middle of the property, right where the pool and house sat. Additionally, there were several ley lines that also intersected smack in the middle of the lot, right through the house.

Ley lines are earth's natural energy lines that, like highways, crisscross the globe, much like longitude and latitude lines. It is thought that they can be used by certain individuals and entities to move about.

Ley lines can also be harmful to your health if you spend a lot of time sitting or lying on one. Where they intersect is very high energy. Humans should not spend a lot of time in those spots. Cats love them. Dogs, not so much. If you want a successful and productive beehive, locate their intersection, and place your hive there. Your bees will thrive. Humans can get sick from long-term exposure to that intense energy.

A very competent psychic medium had identified this issue, placed some boulders, and done some other work to "jump the ley lines" over the house. You can't do much about these natural energy lines other than avoid them. However, by using crystals and other methods, ley lines can be diverted. It's much like diverting water in a river to go around a structure. Their diversion held.

I made additional notes about the spots that I found most troubling and wrapped up the walk-through.

I knew I was in *way* over my head and recognized the need to call in someone to help. Who better than my buddy Sabrina? She has tons of experience in this area. Happily, she was about to be in the region for a workshop and agreed to be available to help in a matter of a week or so. I checked with Socorro, and she eagerly agreed to the appointment.

I briefed Sabrina on the situation, what action the family had taken so far, and my walk-through earlier. She then did a phone consult with Socorro in preparation of her visit.

Like many experienced lightworkers, Sabrina started her work remotely. Tapping into the property, the family, and the larger situation, she immediately knew there were some serious issues with the land. She put together a preliminary plan of action.

We would do a walk-through once we arrived, but the center of the plan would be the house clearing and the Ayni Despacho Ceremony. This ceremony is to put things right and back into balance. Here's a brief description of the ceremony from the article, "What Is A Despacho?."[3]

---

[3] https://thefourwinds.com/blog/shamanism/what-is-a-despacho/

"A despacho is a prayer bundle or offering. For hundreds of years, the Laika (high shamans or wisdom-keepers of the Q'ero lineage of Peru) have used the despacho ceremony for a wide variety of occasions—births, deaths, as an expression of gratitude, to heal physical and emotional ailments, to restore balance and harmony, or when there is a specific request of the spirit world."

Sabrina was in the area for her workshop in the fall of 2015, and we arranged to go to the house after her class ended that Tuesday. We arrived at the property in the early evening. It was already dark. Everything felt different from my daytime walk-through with Robert. As we drove up to the property, it was clear to both of us that *they* knew we were coming. To say we weren't welcomed would be a rather hilarious understatement.

We parked in the driveway and looked at one another. I touched Ohmrah in my pocket, we said some prayers of protection and went into battle.

The entire family had agreed to participate in the ceremony and eagerly greeted us. Since setting up the appointment for the ceremony, the paranormal activity had ramped up its efforts to harm the family and stop us. Activity had skyrocketed, and the family was scared.

McKenzie, the eight-year-old, had gone through about six protection bracelets since I first met the family several months ago. They all had bracelets that broke. She was the one most under attack and couldn't keep hers intact.

All three of the women—mom Socorro, older daughter Bianca, and little McKenzie—were all loaded with powerful gifts, but McKenzie was probably the most powerful. She was a natural medium, albeit undiagnosed or trained in how to control her gifts. Together they were a force. I have zero doubt these three have been soul mates and have spent many lifetimes together.

McKenzie had taken a particular liking to me and always ran over to give me the most amazing hugs. She seemed to feel safe around me, and I felt the need to protect her. I hoped I could live up to her expectations.

I had done some spiritual work in prep for this appointment and felt the need to "dress the part." I have a long, cape-like coat that I've had for many decades. I rarely wear it but absolutely cannot bring myself to get rid of it. It's dramatic and doesn't suit my style any longer. But tonight it was the perfect accessory. It always made me feel special when I wore it. Like I was some high priestess. It was a statement. "Look at me. I'm in control." Yes, it was just what I needed to play the role that night.

We began the walk around the perimeter of the property. Sabrina led the way, the rest of the family and me in tow. Soon into the walk, Sabrina felt sick, just inside the gate to the left of the driveway.

"Ugh." She groaned. "This was a killing field."

We all stopped dead in our tracks as she tapped into the residual energy to see what had happened there. We knew that the land had been a tobacco farm over the last few hundred years, before it was broken up and sold off in lots. She said the owner was a cruel man with many slaves.

When the Civil War ended and emancipation was declared, he didn't respond well.

According to the dead Sabrina was communicating with, the owner and his sons told the slaves they could leave. Distrustful, they gathered their belongings and cautiously started to go. When the group reached this spot, the old man and his sons began firing on the men, women, and children, murdering them all as they tried to flee. This spot was where they were ruthlessly killed. We took a moment to honor their lives and said prayers for them to find peace.

Sabrina also identified numerous ley lines and water veins that ran throughout the property. They seemed a bit odd to her, as they all seemed to unnaturally meet in the center of the lot, where the house and pool were situated. It was almost like they had been manipulated to amplify their energy. And it was not for the betterment of all.

As we rounded the corner of the front of the lot and started down the side toward the back, there was a large tree to our left. There was also a vortex portal. At this point I was out in front of the group slightly. As I came around the side and got close to the tree, a black shadow figure came swooping out of the tree and buzzed me.

I literally ducked, as she was headed directly at my head. I was somehow aware it was a voodoo witch queen. As she rushed by me, she angerly growled, "What the fuck are you doing here, lightworker?"

Sabrina saw it too. We looked at each other and continued on high alert. Yeah, I think they knew we were there.

As we approached the corner of the fence marking the back property line, there was a diagonal ley line *and* an underground water vein that ran directly to the center of the property, right where the house and pool sat. No wonder there was so much activity there!

Sabrina psychically followed the energetic lines away from the property, back to a body of water, likely a pond maybe a mile away. It seemed to be a source of some very bad stuff. It was clear whatever evil was plaguing this land was using these energy lines and the portals to come and go at will. Sabrina advised we put a barrier of salt at that corner, which we did later. It effectively blocked that route into the property. But we had to shut down all the portals and energy highways to affect real protection.

As the group turned the corner, McKenzie was about four feet to my right and slightly ahead of me. Suddenly, she let out a scream. I didn't see anything, but her protection bracelet broke and fell off her wrist. No one was close to her. She freaked out. Everyone gathered around her and tried to calm her down. She grabbed me for protection. Sabrina and I enhanced her protection bubble, and I took my protection bracelet off and put it on her. That made her feel safe again, and despite urging her to head on inside, she wanted to continue the walk and stayed with the group.

As we passed the pool area along the back perimeter, Sabrina mentioned that this area was a real hub of where the entities were coming and going. The water of the pool, the ley lines and the underground water veins were all connected there and created a powerful portal directly under the house and pool.

As we reached the far corner of the property, I suddenly heard horses screaming. Obviously, there were no horses around; this was a residual energy signature. I witnessed an event that involved soldiers and Native Americans in battle. It was bloody and violent, and many on both sides died. Sabrina collaborated my experience.

As we rounded the corner, there was a large bush, and I could tell there was someone (a spirit) hiding there. I was startled but felt no harm from him. Sabrina caught up to me and realized it was an Indian warrior. Part of his face and skull were crushed. I'm sure this is where he died. He lingered after his death, trying to protect the land from the evil, and stayed as a guardian of the land. He seemed to welcome the help.

Other than additional portals, the only other hotspot seemed to be a pile of branches and debris behind the outbuilding. It had accumulated, waiting to be burned. It had a decidedly unsettled feel to it. I'm sure there was something evil lurking, like a rat hiding in the shadows.

The group headed inside, where Sabrina prepared for the Ayni Despacho Ceremony to bring things into right relationship with each other. The entire family participated as she placed the ingredients in the cloth to be sanctified. She began, and as she called on the four directions, her knees buckled, and she was momentarily disoriented. She later explained she was caught off guard by the wickedness of the entity hunting the family. She regained her composure and continued. After the ceremony she performed an exorcism of each member of the family and cut all their ties to this evil.

It was time to bury the completed bundle out on the edge of the property. She and Tim took it to where we had encountered the Native American brave. When they returned inside, she and the women took what remained of the ceremonial wine outside and offered it to Mother Earth.

Things settled down after the ceremony, and the family spent several blissful months feeling safe and peaceful. Then, for whatever reason, evil found its way back onto the property, and the activity flared again. It was disappointing for Socorro, because she was putting in the personal work to let go of her negativity and learning to master her own spiritual gifts. The girls had gone back to school, and the family was generally doing better. They had gotten a little relaxed about their protection protocols. Who knows what happened? For whatever reason, the activity was back.

The entity had already demonstrated it was physically dangerous to the family. Tim, the husband, had been pushed down the stairs. The girls had suffered scratches, and Socorro had been punched in the stomach area numerous times. Something *had* to be done before someone was seriously hurt.

Socorro again reached out to me for help. Still reluctant to do a full-blown exorcism, I agreed to come out and set up some spiritual and psychic protections for the family members.

Sabrina recommended several additional crystals be buried at different spots throughout the property. The family was already back to smudging every day. I agreed to spend a day teaching the family additional advanced techniques they could use for personal psychic defense. I also set up some powerful energetic protections throughout the house.

I spent a lot of time coaching their youngest, McKenzie. As a psychic medium, she was bothered by a lot of dead coming to her during her dream state for help. She was frightened and didn't know how to control her gift.

First, I taught her how to create an auric shield of protection or energy bubble around her. She picked up the technique quickly, and it made her feel much safer. Next, I let her know she had control over her gift. I explained to her that she was under no obligation to help these people unless she chose to. For now, she was too young. Eight years old was way too soon to be trying to navigate the adult issues of the dead seeking help. I had her learn this mantra and use it every night when she was getting ready to go to bed.

"I'm too young. I can't help you. You'll have to find someone else. You must leave now and not return."

I explained she needed to repeat this if she was awakened or had someone seeking her assistance; she should not feel guilty for not helping them right away. She was too young.

I also taught her some simple meditation techniques to control her gifts. Those simple tools and the protection bracelets helped her feel empowered and safe. It did wonders for her anxiety levels. Simply assuring her she wasn't imagining this or going crazy went a long way to help her anxiety.

I finished setting up the rest of the family's protections. Deep down, I knew I was going to have to step up to the task and come back to do the exorcism. My angels had been nudging me for some time now. I knew this was an assignment they weren't going to let go. I finally surrendered to the task and set up a time to return to see what I could do to clear the property.

After committing to the clearing, I set about finding the tools, techniques, and people needed for success. The first member of my lightworker team was Kelly. She's a psychic medium who sees energy and auras. She recommended her daughter, Emma, come along. I was hesitant since Emma was only sixteen at the time. Kelly assured me she had the maturity to handle it, and her skills would be needed. Emma felt compelled to come, feeling she had a mission to be there. I agreed. The final member of the team was Karin, another Reiki master with numerous energy healing protocols under her belt, including sound healing. She was also an expert in working with the Fae. The Fae realm includes fairies, pixies, and other supernatural beings, and elementals.

As soon as the date was set, activity at the property ramped up. Clearly, *they* knew we were coming. I admit to feeling anxious about the decision. But my angelic guides continued to reassure me they would lead me every step of the way. Who was I to doubt them?

A few days before the appointed Thursday, I did a bit of remote work to clear the property. I setup a paper with a rough outline of the property and charted out where the energy and water lines lay. I indicated where we thought the portals were, roughed in the spot for the house, out-buildings, and pool. The pile of brush still had not been burned, so I included that on my chart.

I cleared and programmed some crystals and placed them on the chart to block the energy flow into the property. I placed one over each portal, at the corners of the property and the hot spots. I left it overnight a few days before the clearing.

One of the more interesting things that occurred before the actual clearing was the disturbance I caused during my remote work. I had not been one to put much stock in working remotely. I wasn't sure how that worked, despite learning remote protocols in both Pranic Healing and Reiki training. This cleared up *any* ambivalence I might have had about how effective remote work could be.

Remember I had charted out the property and placed some programmed crystals on it to begin the clearing before the day of the visit? Well, the afternoon before we were heading there, I decided to do some final frequency clearing before taking the crystals off the chart. I headed into my healing room to prepare myself and the area to begin the spiritual work. I took out some of my tuning forks and began to use them over the chart of the property. I declared that I was breaking up negative energy and clearing it away safely. I then took a tuning fork and began to use it directly on the crystals I had placed on the chart. One by one I moved around the crystal grid, vibrating each crystal. I continued to state I was breaking up the negative energy and moving it on safely.

I probably spent about fifteen minutes on the surrounding property and then moved to some of the crystals that were sitting on different parts of the house. Things got intense suddenly, and I became aware I was potentially overwhelming the property. I actually thought, "Oh my! I think I'm about to cause an earthquake!"

I realize how stupid and grandiose that sounds. Using a tuning fork on crystals on a chart of a property thirty miles away could in no way create an earthquake. Or could it? No matter, I got a strong sense I needed to stop. Which I did.

I was curious and just concerned enough that I reached out to Socorro to tell her I was doing some remote work and what I had just experienced. She sounded relieved and shared that a few minutes ago the whole house shook, and she was concerned they were having an earthquake! I swear, you can't make this stuff up and have it be any weirder!

In preparation of the clearing, I also had Socorro take a flat, full-size white cotton sheet and create a magic protection circle. Magic or protection circles exist in many traditions, and this one was to protect the girls during the actual clearing. This one was inspired by the writings of Master Choa Kok Sui from his Pranic Healing book, *Practical Psychic Self-Defense for Home and Office*. In it, he explains this technique is only used under the most extreme cases of psychic attack or the attacker is sending you a powerful negative entity. Yup. Seemed our case fit that description. We would all be busy with our work, and the girls would be home during the clearing, so we would have the girls in the magic circle for their protection.

The instructions were to create four circles on the sheet. Between the fourth and third circle, write out the names of angels. In the next circle, write the names of saints, holy masters, and holy gurus. Finally, between the second and first circle write the holy names of God. Leave the center blank where you remain.

I had them leave ample room in the center to move around. I provided them a list of names to get started with and had the girls put half of them on the sheet before the clearing. I would have them finish the project the day of the clearing.

The girls finished the first part of the magic circle, and McKenzie tried to use it on her bed to sleep the night before the clearing. Nope! It was so intensely powerful it kept her awake. Both girls had their bedrooms upstairs, so they moved the sheet to the hallway between their rooms and that allowed them to sleep yet be protected during the night.

The day of the clearing, I provided lots of colorful markers and stickers and had them spend their time finishing the names of the saints and angels and decorating the sheet with colorful art, doodles, stickers, happy drawings, sayings, and designs.

They were to stay on the sheet the whole time of the clearing. This made it fun, and I felt confident they were protected while we worked. According to Master Choa Kok Sui, no psychic attack or negative beings can penetrate the magic circle with so many holy names.

Kelly was also receiving messages from her angels and spirit guides. They said I needed to find a wand to take with me on the day of the clearing. The only wand I have is a crystal wand I use for my healing work, and it didn't feel like that was the one I needed. The store had several wands, so I looked around, and still none seemed right. I put my trust in my guides to show me the right tool, so I put that worry aside, confident I would find the right wand before we left.

The team was to meet about 8:00 a.m. that Thursday at the store. We all showed up with coffee in hand and the various personal tools we felt compelled to bring with us.

I got there early to continue to search for the right wand to take. We had one I liked that was handmade by one of our local artisans. I grabbed it and tried to intuit if that was the right one. It didn't really feel like it, but I was running out of time and choices. Kelly arrived and asked if I had found the right wand yet. I had to admit I wasn't sure.

I made one last frantic search through the store when my eye caught a walking stick another local artisan had made. It was a long tobacco stick from a local tobacco barn that had been torn down long ago. He had repurposed it into a walking stick. Right after he showed it to me, I had asked if he could incorporate a crystal I had dug. He then reworked it and created a little nook for the crystal to sit in. The stick seemed to jump out at me like, "Take me!" There was no question. *This* was the wand I needed! Looking back on it, I have to wonder if the stick didn't come from the tobacco barn on the very property

103

we were clearing. Of course, I have no way of knowing, but it wouldn't surprise me. Spirit has a way of providing just what you need when you need it.

As we got ready to leave, Kelly asked for a bit more of my plan. To reiterate, I don't do exorcisms, and honestly, I didn't really have a concrete plan to share with her. My angels, especially Holy Archangel Michael, had been providing me with instructions as needed and continued to reassure me they would guide me every step of the way. I could tell Kelly was not as confident when I said, "No solid plan, just doing what they tell me." Talk about stepping out on faith!

She loves me and trusts me and has been working in the spirit realm long enough to know that sometimes you just have to take the leap and know it will be OK. Karin was equally concerned, but she was all in too.

Spirit instructed me to bring some 432 hertz tuning forks, several crystals, salt, the wand, and to have the sacred solfeggio tones loaded on our phones to play during the clearing.

The solfeggio frequencies are part of an ancient six-tone scale used in sacred music for healing and balance. You can find them in beautiful, healing music such as Gregorian chants. The frequencies are thought to impart spiritual blessings when sung or played in harmony. Each tone matches different chakra systems, emotions, and other sacred frequencies. We were planning on using the 963 hertz.

The 963 frequency is associated with awakening intuition and activating the crown chakra, raising positive energy and helping us connect to the God source. It's a very high, sacred frequency, and most lower entities cannot abide it for long. The 432 hertz frequency is often associated with our heart chakra, healing, and unconditional love.

How were we to use them? That remained to be seen. I loaded up my toolbox, and we set off for the job.

We were all quiet on the drive. None of us doubted the magnitude of what we were going to face once there. We weren't afraid. We knew that was the exact emotion and energy this entity fed on. And all of us were experienced spiritual workers, even young Emma, so we kept our emotions in check. I know none of us looked forward to facing this evil. But each of us had been divinely assigned this task, so, like good soldiers, off to battle we marched.

May 26, 2016, was a beautiful, cool spring morning. The sky was bright blue, and puffy clouds meandered overhead. It was the kind of day on which you pack a picnic and go out into nature for a hike. The gorgeous weather belied the darkness and evil that awaited us. As soon as we arrived, we all got the sense the evil entities were waiting for us. And they, too, were ready to fight.

As we pulled into the driveway and got out of the car, I called for another prayer, and we all contributed to our individual and collective energy protection bubble and auric shields.

Socorro was going to join us in the clearing, but Tim was traveling and wouldn't be available. We implemented the plan for the girls by laying the sheet with the magic protection circle on the floor of the garage. The door was open. It was shaded and cool, and they were situated with markers, drinks, and lots of snacks. They would be safe there working on their decorations. With greetings over and the girls safely in the circle, we said additional prayers, grabbed our tools, and began.

It's a good thing my angels came along, because everyone was looking to me for direction. As I shared, I didn't really have a "plan." I was relying on the angels to walk me through step-by-step. I never doubted they would, but it was a relief when I immediately knew what to do first. Whew!

We all turned on our phones and played the sacred solfeggio 963 hertz frequency. We all agreed to play it consistently while we worked. We sounded a bit like high-pitched angry bees walking around! The next thing the angels had me do was to resalt the energetic highway leading in from the distant pond in the corner of the property. I had brought some chunks of salt, and we did a ceremony at that corner of the fence to stop the entities from using that route.

Next, I was instructed to start closing the portals, one by one. These portals had been created by someone or something in a way that their energy was very chaotic and therefore difficult to pinpoint exactly where they were from moment to moment. They kept jumping slightly from one spot to the next, which made it almost impossible to find and close them.

Archangel Michael had me bring a 432 hertz chime to each of the entire team. We located the portal closest to the corner of the property we had just salted. Forming a triangle around the portal, we began to chime in unison. It became clear that the angels were having us stabilize the portal so it could be found and subsequently closed. Clever!

After about five minutes, we all felt the portal settle down and remain in one spot. I picked up the tobacco walking stick "wand" and used it to close the portal. Honestly, I didn't know how to do this. And I don't remember what I said. Clearly spirit was speaking through me. I was merely the channel. I had to suspend any desire to maintain my human persona. I felt a bit like Moses, raising the wand skyward and making bold sweeping pronunciations like, "In the name of Jesus, I command you to close." I admit to feeling a bit silly and self-conscious. But it was clear this was the angels working through me, and I simply needed to stay out of their way. I put my ego down and did as I was told.

After our first success, we branched off into teams. Emma felt strongly about the large fir tree close to where I had encountered the voodoo witch queen. She headed over there to begin her work. Kelly stayed close to Emma while Socorro, Karin, and I moved about the property closing the portals using the same procedure. One by one we stabilized and closed them all. This cut off the routes these entities had been using into and out of the property.

Emma is an old soul and was way beyond her age in maturity. She was able to connect to the voodoo queen. It seems she had not always been evil. She was from Haiti and the healer for the

107

slaves there on the plantation. She was aware of the portals and, while alive, had tried to close them but wasn't strong enough. In death her soul had been taken over by the evil that tainted the land and everyone on it. Emma worked with her on forgiveness and was able to pass her over into the light. One soul at rest.

Over by where the battle between the Native Americans and the soldiers had taken place, we cleared the residual energy and balanced the area. The brave that protected the area joined us and agreed to continue to stand guard over the land. We offered to help him pass over, but he elected to stay for as long as he was needed.

The area where the slaves were massacred was also cleared and balanced, but none of us sensed many souls were lingering there. I suspected they were still being held captive over by the pool area. That was where the entity was the strongest. We would work with those souls later.

As we walked back toward the rear of the property, I got a phone call. I had forgotten to put my cell phone on do not disturb. Rats! It was my older sister, CJ. I will speak more about her and this situation later. For now, I mention this occurrence because she had been plagued by a dark entity that had tortured our family for generations. I was aware of its presence and was taking precautions to avoid it jumping to me after she passed.

I did answer the call, because she was already very sick, and I was afraid my work was having some blowback on her. I halfway expected a demon to answer on the other end of the line!

Happily, that wasn't the case. I know I frightened her a bit by my tone and abrupt ending of the call, but I didn't know what else to do.

It's well known that entities can use electronics as portals and highways for moving around. I learned later what a big mistake I had made answering the call.

Karin works closely with the fae, and as we moved about the property, she enlisted all the elementals interested in clearing and balancing the land. She reported that one of the trees on the back side of the property literally took a sigh of relief after we closed the portal near it. We still didn't have any birds or squirrels on the property, but they were being increasingly sighted along the fence line. A good sign of progress.

Closing the portals and balancing the land took several hours and was exhausting work. We were done with most of it, except for the pool area. I knew it would be a big project, so we all took a break and had some food and drink.

The girls joined us in the kitchen, and, after we were refreshed, we walked with them as they returned to the protection circle on the garage door floor. Once they were safe, we headed outside through the open garage door and walked around to the front of the house. As we headed toward the backyard and the pool. A car unexpectedly drove up into the driveway, and Socorro panicked.

"Oh no! I forgot one of Bianca's friends was coming over this afternoon!" She was shaken at this development. I put my hands on her shoulder and calmed her down.

109

"We have the angels protecting us," I reminded her. "If this friend has showed up, she has a part to play in this healing."

Socorro started to calm down a bit. "OK, OK. She comes over a lot and knows all about the paranormal stuff going on."

"She will be safe in the circle with the girls," I said. "Clearly, she is here because of her experiences with this. She will be cleared of any energetic cords, so relax. It's all good."

Reassured, Socorro headed over to get the friend situated and to explain what was going on. She was happy to comply and joined Bianca and McKenzie on the magic protection circle.

As the rest of the team headed around the house toward the backyard pool, we checked each of the portals and areas we had worked on in the morning. Everything was holding. The portals remained closed, and the land felt considerably lighter.

Socorro caught up to us as we were about to reach the pool. I felt something rush by me. Kelly jumped, Karin squealed, and Socorro screamed and dissolved into sobs, clearly terrified. The evil entity we had been hunting just ran past us! I felt it go by, but I didn't see it with my human eyes. The rest of the team did.

Things were getting real, and we were all shaken by the encounter. I calmed Socorro and reminded everyone that the entity fed off fear. We had to stay in the frequency of love or above if we wanted to have a chance of defeating it.

Deep breaths, prayers, and reinforcing our energy shields did the trick. Once we all regained our composure, I forced it out of the briar pile, where it had taken shelter. We corralled it in the pool area and armed with our chimes, surrounded the area.

I think Karin was the first to see one of its minions crawling on the wooden deck around the pool and gasped. It was weakened from all the work we were doing and deprived of its energy source of fear, the portals, ley lines and water veins. It was trying to make it out of the property via the large portal under the pool. We had no intention of letting it escape. Using the chimes, 963 hertz tones, prayers, and the Ho'oponopono chant, "I love you, I'm sorry, please forgive me, thank you," we immobilized it, and I was able to send it back to wherever it had originated.

One more down.

Imagine the team spread out around the pool, each of us praying, chanting, and using the tones. Happily, there were no close neighbors wondering what in the world was going on over there! I'm sure we were quite the sight.

Archangel Michael had me close the unstable portal using the methods we employed on the other portals. Soon after closing the portal beneath the pool, I became aware of a number of trapped souls close to the house to my left. I think they were a collection of many that had died on the property, including the murdered slaves.

Archangel Michael then instructed me to open a new, stable portal to the light over the pool. In loud authoritative commands, I raised the wand in my right hand and commanded a portal be opened. I don't remember what I said next, but it was Archangel Michael speaking in light language. Now there was a way for any trapped souls to move out of bondage and into the light.

I commanded all of them to "jump into the portal" and be free. Several moved quickly but, some remained hesitant. At that point, I remember saying something like, "OK everybody. Let's go. Hurry up! Time to cross over."

This was a side of me that neither I nor my team had ever seen! Clearly, I was still being a channel.

I sensed about thirty or forty souls cross over. Once I was sure no more needed to go, I closed that portal. I also sealed the area right under the pool. We felt confident the main evil entity had been cast out. Ready to relax, we started to move toward the back door, and we collectively realized it had escaped. Into the house. Oh great!

Quickly we put up shields around the house so it couldn't get out. We had it cornered. We just had to find exactly where it was in the house.

That didn't take long. We found it in the upper outside corner of McKenzie's bedroom. Our shields were holding. It was trapped. We gathered in a half circle around the foot of the bed, keeping any escape route blocked. The team followed whatever inspiration spirit was providing them. Some prayed, chimed the tuning forks, chanted. We were still all playing the 963 hertz frequency.

We had it cornered. Now what? Archangel Michael whispered in my ear.

"Nothing can resist the sweetness of unconditional God Love." —Archangel Michael

I immediately knew to use the Ho'oponopono chant, "I love you, I'm sorry, please forgive me, thank you."

I told the team the instructions I had just been given. They showered the entity with the love frequency, each in their own way.

I began singing the chant over and over, sending pure love. The entity sneered at me and growled. "If you think you can defeat me by singing, you are a fool."

I continued to sing, projecting love as purely as I could while it sneered and twisted in the corner. I cleared my heart of any judgment or fear, sending nothing but love. No conditions.

It took several minutes, maybe ten or so, before I saw any progress. When I reached that sweet spot of unconditional love, I began weeping. I felt the entity soften. It went from being a black blob in the corner to more of a human form. It then started to dissipate like smoke. Then it was gone.

Archangel Michael was right. Nothing can resist the sweetness of God's unconditional love.

The team collectively stopped chanting and praying, as if on cue, as the entity disappeared. We were all crying. We had cleared it!

We took a short break and collected the girls to do one final walk around the property. It was quiet. Clear. Everything in the yard felt alive again! Karin saw a fir tree take a deep breath! There were birds in the trees. And they were singing! A squirrel even ran by us as if to say, "Hi!" After five years of living there, this was the first time the family saw any birds or squirrels. It was a real celebration of life.

No one was under the illusion that we had fixed the problem and conquered evil. All we had managed to do was clear the property, balance the energy, and shut down the portals in and out of the property. Like any relentless pest, it would take constant vigilance to keep the area clear.

But at least for now, the family could live in peace, free of fear, and sell the property. No doubt they, too, had been a part of the healing. Socorro shared with me that they moved from California for one of Tim's jobs. The contract on the original house they bought fell through at the last minute. They had purchased this property sight unseen out of desperation for a quick solution on a place to live.

Looking back on it, it would seem all of us had several life lessons to learn from this. First, how to heal ourselves and how to manage our gifts. Second, how to recognize evil and not tolerate it in our lives. Third, how to hold a space for light and love.

Make no mistake. The evil there still exists. Whatever it is, it has been there for a *very* long time and will likely always be there. Some land is just not a place where humans should try to live.

All we did was carve out a space where evil was not welcome or tolerated. We all learned how to employ numerous techniques to get it out and keep it out. At the end of the day, the most powerful tool was love. The low frequencies of misery, anger, hate; evil, are incompatible with the high frequency of love.

I now understand my divine assignment wasn't an exorcism. It was an exercise to learn how to hold the space for love, despite overwhelming evil. Love is always the answer.

To live there with any safety and peace of mind, the family had to continue their daily routines of smudging and burning incense. They kept a constant eye on their own emotions and inner peace. Even the girls learned how to recognize when the family was slipping into dissonance. Socorro shared that young McKenzie would walk through the door some days and announce, "Mom! We need to smudge. Right now!"

They all watched the yard carefully. If the birds were chirping and squirrels were darting about, they knew the barriers were holding. As soon as it got quiet, they would resalt the perimeter and reinforce the barriers around the property. All the personal work the family did to heal themselves individually and collectively allowed them to live with peace of mind—even knowing evil was ready to take over any time they strayed from harmony.

The family was finally able to sell the property and move to a new home. Socorro was concerned they would bring the evil with them. They had been personally exorcised during the despacho ceremony and learned how to cut energetic cords. So I wasn't too worried about that. I did advise them to put the magic circle sheet in the hallway where the movers would be hauling furniture and boxes out. I had her set the intention that any and all energy, attachments, or entities that were not of the light could *not* pass the barrier of the magic circle.

I told her to repeat that process when they brought the items into their new house. She placed the sheet on the floor and set the intention that nothing could cross the barrier into the new home. I had her then bless the sheet and burn it in a ceremony that released anything that didn't belong on the earth plane or wasn't of the light.

I'm happy to report all negative paranormal activity has ceased for the family, and they are enjoying their new home.

They did a full disclosure with the family purchasing the old property. The purchasing family was told of the events but said they didn't believe in all that hooey, and it was perfect for their family.

I haven't checked into whether or not they still reside there, but we found out they began experiencing negative activities a few months into living there.

But Socorro and her family were finally at peace. Evil had been kept in its place. Whew!

Or Maybe Not

Remember the phone call I took from my sister while we were clearing the property? Yeah, don't ever do that, my friends. I had neglected to protect my cell phone and, sure enough, evil found its way in through my electronics.

About a week after the clearing, I was finishing up some marketing posts on social media at about 9:30 p.m. My husband was at work, and I was working late that night. Ding. I got a notification of a direct message. I checked and it was one of my husband's male relatives. This is someone I don't know very well and have never chatted with on social media. Odd. OK, maybe something was up in the family. I responded. He started chatting me up, and I immediately suspected he was drunk or high or both. I have personally only met this man three or four times in my life, and we don't live close to one another.

I was polite in my responses, but terse. After about four exchanges back and forth, he sent two pictures. Of his boy-parts. Yikes! What?! Where did *that* come from? It seemed completely out of the blue considering our non-relationship. I was baffled.

I immediately blocked him. Unsettled, I tried to figure out what had just happened. And then it dawned on me. Oh…I got the message.

I realized *he* hadn't sent the message. His addictions had left him wide open to anything that wanted to use him. The poor man was a channel for the evil we had just battled at Socorro's place. The message was loud and clear.

"Fuck you!" or "I can still fuck with you," or "I'm going to fuck with you." Not exactly sure, but I know "fuck you" was certainly a portion of the message.

I felt a little apprehension and fear rise in my throat. Had this evil entity found me? Was I in danger? I did some deep breathing and tried to calm down. I am well aware the emotional frequency of fear is what it feeds on. While it's natural to have a reaction, I knew I had to get it under control and retrieve my peace of mind.

After a few moments of breathing, praying, and sending healing to this family member, I felt the presence of Archangel Michael near me.

> *Return to the place of love. Bathe in the light and joy of knowing you are not alone and [are] well protected. Fear cannot exist in the presence of love.* —
> Archangel Michael

His reassurance was all it took for me to calm down. For me, the lesson remains the same. Evil has always and will always exist. It's not my job, nor is it possible, to eliminate all evil. The answer is balance. On what side of the street do you want to spend your time and energy? When you choose light and love, you can observe the darkness and acknowledge it is there. Your responsibility is to choose whether to live in lightness or darkness and then keep your light shining.

It took a few moments, but I was able to bring my emotions back into harmony with love and no longer felt any fear. Quite the opposite. I felt powerful. I needed no sword, no crystals, no magic incantation. I needed only love. And that I could manage. I will choose to hold the space around me for light and love.

Interdimensional Being Crashes through Our Bedroom Window

Things had been going well at the store and for me personally. I was making progress with my health, losing weight, and making connections with my spirit guides. But it's not much of a story if everything is going well and it ends there, is it? Of course not! Here's why I call out the date October 14, 2017.

It's 1:30 a.m. Of course I don't know what time it is, because my husband and I are peacefully asleep. That is until there is a loud crash, and the mini blinds on one of the windows are pulled down. The dog starts barking, and we both bolt upright in bed.

"What the…" Let me just say, I would never make it as a James Bond type. You know how, out of a dead sleep, he leaps out of bed, weapon in hand, clear minded and ready for combat? Yeah. Not me. I'm startled. I'm confused and dull witted.

Robert grabbed his flashlight and immediately identified the source. The bottom pane of our vinyl window on the far side of the bedroom had fallen out of its track, pulling the blinds with it as it crashed to the floor.

I repeat, "What the…"

"It's just the window," he announced.

Granted, the windowpane was not locked in place, but we've had these windows for a decade. Not once has any of them had one of their panes randomly come out of its track and fall to the ground. There was no wind that night. In fact, it was a lovely, starry night.

Naturally, I was startled, but the entirety of the situation hadn't dawned on me yet. "OK, it's just the window," I say to myself. Robert picked up the pane and put it back into place. He was up, so he headed to the bathroom. I was still in bed and very unsettled. Something didn't feel right. At all. I lay back down, but I was now wide awake.

The ceiling right above the head of our bed is angled as it reaches the highest part of the ceiling. As I laid there listening to the dog barking wildly downstairs, I watched a small ball of light track along the ceiling from my right, over the top of me to the left of the bed (where I sleep). At first I thought it was Robert coming back out of the bathroom with his flashlight. It was a little weird for the beam of a flashlight, but that's what I thought. I sat up to check. He was still in the bathroom and the door was closed.

I remember saying out loud, "Well, that's not good."

I knew instinctively it was one of my guardians. It was a light being I saw tracking across the ceiling. I knew there had to be a good reason for my guardians to be so visible and in such a hurry. It was more than the windowpane falling out of the window for no reason. That realization shot through me like lightning.

Robert returned to bed, and I decided to use the bathroom myself. I quickly got up and headed there to pee and gather my senses. I was becoming increasingly unsettled. The dog had settled down a bit. As I returned to the bedroom, I stepped into the area next to the side of the bed where I sleep and completely freaked out!

I walked right into whatever or whoever had crashed through the window moments earlier. It was like walking into a pressurized room. It felt so weird! I was disoriented and frightened.

I do this vocalization when I'm having a nightmare, it sounds like what you see ghosts do, this "ooh, ooh, ooh" kind of moan. Yep. That's the only thing I could manage in that moment.

Then I yelled, "Something's in the room!" Robert was now sitting bolt upright again in bed. I ran over to his side and stood behind him. Like he would protect me from this invisible whatever that had invaded our space! I was half crying with fear. Poor Robert. He doesn't freak out easily, but I was totally freaking him out.

It's not like you can check the handbook on what to do in these situations. That's why it's good to be prepared. My training kicked in. Love. The frequency of love. I had just cleared some seriously evil stuff a few months ago with nothing more than prayer and love.

I'd been attacked numerous times during my dream state. I knew I had power by asserting myself and claiming the space for love. OK. Get control of my emotions. If it *was* evil, it would become more powerful if I was fearful. Deep breaths.

Robert and I recited the Lord's Prayer. Several times. I declared myself as being of pure source light and commanding the entity or evil being to remove itself. I claimed the space for light and love and declared anything that wasn't from the highest source for the highest good of all was not allowed in this space. I called on the angels. I commanded in the name of Jesus for this thing to leave. "Get out!"

After a few minutes, we both settled down, the dog had stopped barking, and the area seemed clear. To say we were wide awake would be a slight understatement!

We headed downstairs to take the dog out. With flashlights in hand, Robert, the pup, and I headed out front. There was nothing obvious in the front yard or in the driveway. At the end of the driveway, I was called to look back at the house.

"Shine your light on the roof above our bedroom," I said. As we stood at the end of the driveway, his beam illuminating that spot, I saw it. Crouched there on the roof, just above the bedroom, I saw something like a stick figure. It was dark, with a long, spindly torso, arms, and legs. It had one "knee" and one "hand" on the roof. The other hand was shielding his "eyes" from Robert's flashlight.

Somehow, I wasn't afraid. Completely weirded out—but not fearful. I looked right at it. I knew that it knew I saw it. Telepathically I said, "I see you. You know you don't belong here. You must leave." And it did.

Once back inside, Robert took the couch with the dog, and I slept in the recliner for the remainder of the night. As you can imagine, I wasn't going back up to the bedroom until daylight!

The next morning, we gathered our courage and went back upstairs to the bedroom. Things always seem less scary in the daylight. Robert went about picking up the mini blind and putting it back in place, while I cautiously returned to my side of the bed to see if that weird disturbance remained.

Happily, it had dissipated, and the energy upstairs was almost back to normal. I was good with that and quickly headed downstairs for breakfast. I would deal with it later.

I honestly didn't know what had happened. I knew *something* or *someone* had come crashing through the window. It made its way over and stood beside my side of the bed, and my guardians were on it. I had seen something not of this earth plane on my roof. In the bright light of day, it didn't really feel like I had been in danger or that this entity had evil intent. It was just one of those profoundly weird and inexplicable encounters. Definitely an episode of high strangeness.

I immediately contacted a few of my most trusted friends. Naturally, I related the episode to Sabrina. She picked up on it being an interdimensional being, young, running for its life. Something had been chasing it, and it saw my light (love). It intuitively knew to go toward that light, that it would be safe. Her assessment was that it had literally crashed through a portal (my window) to escape whatever had been chasing it. Yikes! I don't want to know what was chasing it!

Two additional sources I trust agreed. Someone had crashed through a portal while trying to escape being chased. One thought it was a shadow being, the other felt it was an interdimensional being.

After meditating on it, it felt more like an interdimensional being. I got the vision of it crashing through the pane of the window like a football player diving into a tackle. Then it hit the wall just inside the room and did a somersault due to the momentum, ending up at the middle of the room. After I got up to use the bathroom, it made its way over to my side of the bed. When I returned, I basically walked into it, or at least into the disturbance it was causing in the atmosphere.

I spent a lot of time cleaning up the energetic mess from the incident. I smudged the room and closed the portal. God knows I certainly didn't want whatever was chasing this thing to find a way through! I cleared the spot on the wall where it had "hit," smudged and cleared the bed and area all around it. I did this a few times before I was satisfied everything was cleared.

I'll admit in hindsight it never occurred to me this thing might have needed my help. I just sent it packing. I did feel a bit guilty for not asking who it was or it wanted. But my advisors reassured me to keep the contact to a minimum. OK. I can do that. In any case, it was reassuring to see physical evidence of my guardians and angels when the light appeared over my head that night. I feel very protected.

For additional protection against psychic attack, I placed amethyst crystals at the corners of the bed between the box springs and mattress. I programmed them as protection crystals to form a protection barrier bubble around the bed. I'm happy to report that, since that night, no further incidents with beings crashing through the window have occurred!

Let's Talk about Witches

All my life, I've been terrified of witches and witchcraft. I remember being in a bookstore as a young teen and seeing a book lying on the sales table with a pentagram and the title *Witchcraft*. A bolt of fear ran through my body. I couldn't even be close to it. I felt something terrible would happen if I touched it.

I'm sure a lot of my fear was my Protestant upbringing, pop culture, and movies. "Witches are bad! They have prominent warts with long bristly whiskers protruding. They all have bad teeth and skin and pointy hats, and do horrible things to people, especially children!"

Of course now that I've actually explored what Wicca and witchcraft stand for, I have lost my irrational fears. I have several employees who are practicing Wiccan witches, as are many of my customers and clients.

But my fear at the time seemed to be deeper than that. Even as a young person, I suspected I had been executed for being a witch in a prior lifetime. It had a ring of injustice to it, as I was falsely accused by a jealous relative.

Alcoholism, smoking, obesity, and lots of negative family drama had plagued my family for generations. I began to wonder if there was a family "demon" hanging out, tormenting us and feeding off the negativity. I also felt I had some responsibility for introducing it and therefore clearing it.

I did a past-life regression a few years ago, in part to see if this memory had any basis to it. During the session, I remembered four past lifetimes. Two involved extraterrestrials. One memory seemed irrelevant to that question. But the last lifetime I remembered directly answered my question about the family demon.

Let Me Tell You the Story of Thomas

This memory took me to a lifetime about five hundred years ago. I found myself observing a cabin in the woods that's classic to most fairy tales involving witches. I saw a young boy, maybe twelve or so, outside the cottage, peering in through a dirty window. He was scrawny, hungry, and it was clear he had been banished from coming inside. I came to learn I was known as Thomas during this lifetime.

My mother had died when I was even younger, and I was watching my grandmother working inside the cottage. She was a wholly unpleasant woman, who made no attempt to hide her contempt for me and her anger for having to become my caretaker. She worked from cabinets lined with bottles of herbs and jars filled with who knows what. She scurried about making up potions and medicine bags. My job was to take them into the village and deliver them to the person who had ordered them, collect the money, and bring it back to her.

Like all children, I longed for love and acceptance and happily complied to any of her demands. I wanted to learn her craft, but she had no intention of teaching me anything. I was the Middle Ages version of a troubled youth.

When she died, I eagerly took over the family business of concocting healing brews, potions, and medicine bags. The problem was I didn't have the knowledge and skill she had. Soon enough, I was in trouble when one of my remedies failed and the infant daughter of a villager died. They angerly demanded their money back and justice. I had no intention of accepting responsibility or returning their money.

An angry mob showed up at the cottage, again demanding justice for the family and accusing me of witchcraft. I was defiant. They set fire to the cottage. As I died, I screamed curses at them and asked for a demon to come forth to avenge my death.

As I came out of the session, we looked at one another, and I said, "Hmmm, I think I see the problem!"

Karma. Geesh. Well, isn't that just great?

I think the grandmother in my past lifetime was my older sister CJ this time around. At the time of my past-life regression, my sister was extremely sick and close to passing. I had suspected we did indeed have a familial problem for a while. I was fairly sure it was camping out with CJ this lifetime. I also suspected that once that "host" was gone, it would need another. I thought it would likely try to jump to another family host at her death.

I didn't think it would be me. I felt it was a chaos entity. These lower entities need lots of drama and negativity to sustain themselves. I had done enough personal work by that point that I felt relatively safe. Not much self-induced drama in my life. I wasn't so sure about some of the other members of the family becoming its target. I felt responsible to ensure that didn't happen. After all, if I indeed had unleased this thing, it was my responsibility to put it back where it belonged.

So how the heck do I do that? It was time to consult with experts.

Luckily, I thought of my friend who works under the name of Azrael. I contacted him, and he agreed to take the job. He works remotely and on different dimensional planes that allow him to reach out to spirit and do his work. I brought him up to date, and he went to work. It seems I had some of it right.

Here's his report:

> Thomas and Maurydex
>
> I, Azrael, called upon the entity Maurydex to arrange a meeting to discuss the ongoing relationship she had with Susan and CJ throughout time. We agreed to talk at a place known to Maurydex and met at CJ's house. When I arrived, the entity was not materially present, but the essence was, and soon after I asked for it to take shape. The entity did so, transforming into what can only be described as a hybrid between a hedgehog and a wolf: long, drawn face, limbs that were spindly but muscular like a wolf, and prickly quills all over its back. Maurydex's demeanor was one of

curiosity and anxiety; she did not know the nature of this visit. I sat on a nearby chair, while she sat on the ground under the hearth of the house.

I began initially by requesting the entity give me her name, and that I had been given permission to not only contact her but to aid in her transition (if agreed upon) away from Susan and possibly CJ. Maurydex was curious why this was happening, as she didn't see the immediate issues at hand. We talked for some time about the very nature of why she was even in this timeline and what was the end goal of her work. She agreed to travel back to the time when Thomas was creating the conditions for her appearance into this realm.

We stepped into the very forest near the cabin where Thomas and his grandmother lived. At first impression I would say this was late 1600s. I noticed that the grandmother had cared for some of the creatures in the woods at the cabin, including a wounded hedgehog (presumably how Maurydex became known as a similar being).

Thomas was a young, and his mother had been ill. Thomas had heard of a Native American healer in the woods by the name of Bobcat. This woman had been outcast by her tribe for her "dark magic," which she had used against a warring tribe, but it had backfired. He began to learn not only natural healing but of some of the spiritual work she had continued. It was then that he believed he could combine them to help his community with their sick people.

Unfortunately, his early work did not go well, resulting in the immediate deaths of a few people. Outraged, the town gathered outside his cabin and set a fire to kill him while inside.

At this time, we observed Thomas's emotions and thoughts and could see things through Thomas's view. His anger, anxiety, depression, pride, remorse, and clouded judgment brought about an agreement with chaos to bring about a spirit that would avenge him, to make these people realize their grave mistake.

As the burning house came crashing down on him, that entity was brought forth, attacking the folk around the cabin and going back to the town with them. For years, Maurydex was allowed to make the sick and wounded from the town quickly spiral into death.

After this point, Maurydex had completed the debt to Thomas but didn't have a resting spot or agreement to return back to spirit. She stayed within family members until this point in time, finding CJ as her current host. This kept a connection to Susan, since they were related by blood. I estimate that the sisters' shared abdominal issues are a result of Maurydex and her base nature.

I called upon the angel Zadkiel to assist in the healing of both of the sisters, while I and Maurydex cleared the quills she had left behind. I then traveled back with Maurydex to the current time and asked her if she would like to transition back to spirit either now or when CJ leaves this Earth. Maurydex was very agreeable to leaving when CJ died and showed signs of rest and satisfaction. I then made it clear that Susan does not want to be a new host or have any ties for future arrangements. Maurydex agreed to this and took an oath in spirit to be at peace with Susan as well as Thomas.

Wow! It seems it wasn't a demon but more of an interdimensional elemental. That was good news! Demons cannot be negotiated with. Elementals can. It started to make so much sense to me. I (Thomas) had summoned this entity and given it a job to do, but I hadn't set an end to the contract or a way to return to its place of origin.

Side note. Let this be a lesson not to dabble!

OK, it sounded like we had a solid plan to amend my past-life mistake and avoid any future chaos. Azrael created a Spirit of Accord agreement for me to agree to and a ceremony to burn it. Here's the agreement:

Spirit of Accord
Written and Sealed by Azrael,
On behalf of Susan and Maurydex
An agreement has been made by these parties,
witnessed by Heaven above and Earth below,
That the entity Maurydex has severed all and
any ties with Susan,
And to which Susan has also relieved Maurydex
of any debts owed, and any spiritual contracts
placed in both time and space.
This is an attestation to their mutual declaration
of peace to one another and shall be found
binding throughout all of Creation.

Nothing Is Ever Simple

You must realize by now nothing is as simple as it appears on the surface.

It was early November, and my sister CJ lay on her deathbed. Something told me that Maurydex wasn't going to go home quite as easily as she had led us to believe. I began to doubt her commitment to return to her place of origin, and I put up my guard.

Around Thanksgiving, CJ's estranged daughter came to visit her before she died to try and heal some of their troubled relationship. There had been decades of anger and hurt on both sides, and I had my serious doubts about how this would unfold. She arrived unannounced and made her way to visit CJ at the nursing home. This could have gone either way. There was an equal chance CJ would have a fit of anger and throw her out of the room—or give into love and open her heart to heal. Thank God she opened her heart and welcomed her daughter with open arms.

During her stay in town, my niece and her husband came over to our home for dinner one night. I told her about the familial entity and what I had done up to that point. I also shared with her my new concerns that things wouldn't necessarily go as smoothly as I first imagined.

Dinner conversation revolved around numerous paranormal and spiritual subjects. She has strong gifts of her own, albeit untapped. We were talking about the power of negative energy and how to protect oneself as we finished dinner. I got up to clear the plate from her spot, and as I stood there, I heard a loud pop.

Directly behind me was a cabinet where I keep napkins and other dinner items. On top I had a glass burning bowl. The glass on the bowl was about three-eighths of an inch thick, and it was perhaps one and a half inches deep. It was elevated on an ornate metal stand with curved feet. The bowl resembled a glass pie plate. I had about half an inch of salt and a number of crystals laid out in a protection grid. In the center I had placed a six-inch standing polished quartz crystal. It was about two inches in diameter.

Hearing the loud pop right behind me, I turned to discover the bowl had broken. The crystal point had toppled over, and the salt was pouring out the bottom of the bowl onto the top of the cabinet. Mind you, no one had touched the bowl. I had my back to it.

Startled, I examined it closer. There was a chunk of glass directly below the center crystal that looked like it had been blown out, sending the crack outward to the edge of the bowl and toppling the crystal.

I had a very strong sense it was Maurydex. And it wasn't a friendly exchange. The burning bowl and crystals in it had been programmed as diversionary crystals, meaning they would attract negative energy like a lightning rod away from me and channel the energy downward to Mother Earth to be grounded and transmuted.

We were all a bit freaked. Prayers and protection bubbles went up. I had seen crystals break and had a lot of experience with my protection bracelets taking the hit for myself and clients, but this was a whole different level.

I knew I needed to revisit the situation with Maurydex's leaving upon CJ's death. I told Azrael my new concerns that Maurydex may not have been completely honest. I felt she had no intention of returning to her point of origin and would instead try to jump to a new host at CJ's death. I told him I wanted her to leave before CJ died. Maurydex made it clear to him she had no intention of leaving early. That matter was between CJ and her, not her and me. If CJ's soul wanted her to leave early, she would.

I knew that would not be a possibility. I had never mentioned any of this to my sister, and at this point, she was hallucinating and often delirious, so this was certainly NOT something to dive into. I would have to communicate with her higher self and leave her earthly personality out of it.

Entities from chaos and chaotic dimensions can be expected to do what they do—create chaos. It seemed Maurydex was sowing chaos again. I asked Azrael to revise the Spirit Accord. Here's how I had him amend it:

Spirit of Accord
Written and Sealed by Azrael,
On behalf of Susan and Maurydex
An agreement has been made by these parties,
witnessed by Heaven above and Earth below,

That the entity Maurydex has severed all and any ties
with Susan,
And to which Susan has also relieved Maurydex of any debts owed, and any spiritual contracts placed in both time and space.
Maurydex will transition back to her origin when Susan's sister, CJ, departs from this earthly plane. Until such time, Maurydex will discontinue any form of chaotic energy transferal and be held accountable for any further energetic release until her transition to source.
This is an attestation to their mutual declaration of peace to one another and shall be found binding throughout all of Creation.

Inspired by my spirit guides (or perhaps wisdom from ancient lifetimes ago), I performed a ceremony to "seal the deal" with Maurydex. Mind you, I had no experience in any of this. I have to assume my guardian angels instructed me. This is how I finally closed this chapter and brought balance where I had sown chaos so long ago.

Sealing the Deal
I took a ritual salt bath to cleanse my energy and afterward handwrote the contract. I set up a fire pit in the backyard and took some sage and the contract outside. I did a short meditation and apologized to any and all throughout time that I, or my actions, had harmed. I prayed for forgiveness. I apologized to Maurydex for calling her in from her home and declared our contract

to be canceled. I gave instructions for her to return to her place of origins and to not return.

I then pricked my finger, letting a drop of blood fall on the contract. I smeared it to sign it and set the contract on fire over the pit. I prayed for and commanded this time of chaos and trouble come to an end—that it be transmuted and healed. I'd sealed it in my blood. After the ceremony, I felt secure that this chapter in my soul's existence had come to an end. I no longer feared that Maurydex would try to stay earthbound and make a jump to anyone else in the family. And she didn't.

I filed this experience under "let this be a lesson to you about calling forth entities and curses!" Just don't!

The Angels Come to Escort Her to The Light

About a month later, it was clear my sister was very close to dying. I had been around death when my mother passed but not present the actual moment of transition. I was there with my sister as she passed on Christmas morning in December of 2018.

She had been very sick for a very long time, and her physical body frequencies had been very low. She was one of those people that was so sick you wonder how they are even alive. People would ask me, "How's your sister?" and I would say, "She's still alive."

It was her strong will to live that kept her spirit resident in her physical body, which, I'm sad to say, she had not taken good care of at all.

When she hit that spot where her physical body couldn't accommodate her spirit any longer, she was transported from the nursing home to the hospital ER. Her husband and I each held one of her hands as she lay in a catatonic state moments before her physical body died. Even though she couldn't speak, we knew that she knew we were with her. In about twenty minutes, she became resigned to her imminent passing and surrendered to the inevitable.

Her physical life was no longer sustainable. At the moment she died and her soul separated, I felt angelic presences, and we both heard the angels' choir. It was truly magical. She wasn't particularly religious, but the angels were right there. It was such a comfort to her husband!

It was like, "Wow." I talk about this stuff all the time, but I'm human, and so it's really wonderful to get validation that all this stuff that you've been talking actually happened to you!

And that's what the angels have told me to tell you about death: that your soul never dies, and there are always angels there to help you through the transition.

CJ had been so sick for so long; it actually was a blessing when she passed. There was nothing anyone could do to prevent it or lessen her pain or make her comfortable. To see someone suffering like that was truly torture.

It was just before 10:00 a.m. Christmas morning when she passed. The staff in the ER and EMTs that had brought her were all ready for her husband and I to be devastated. There she was, dying on Christmas morning. Christmas would never be the same. Some tears fell, of course, but when we left the room, the staff didn't know exactly how to respond. They all expressed their sorrow.

But that's not how either her husband or I felt in that moment. We had just been part of a miracle. Angels had escorted our loved one as she departed her earthly body. Her suffering had ended.

They were rather shocked to see we both were rather joyful. Yes, it was sad to say goodbye to her familiar body, but we knew the part of her that never dies, her soul, was in good hands.

I put the staff at ease about it by expressing Christmas morning was a glorious day to die. Think about it. A large portion of the globe is in a happy place because of the meaning of Christmas.

"Best to go when everyone's in a good mood." I said, "It's a good day to travel!"

Surprised, the staff relaxed. We shattered their thinking that her death meant the holiday would forever be ruined for us. I reassured them it was quite the opposite. I was choosing to celebrate my sister going out in style. Why *not* pick one of the holiest, happiest days of the year? Bravo, CJ!

I had zero trepidation that Maurydex hadn't returned to her point of origin. I knew that chapter was closed.

You'll be happy to know, CJ has visited with me several times since her passing. The first time was about a week after her physical death. One of the mediums was in the store that day, and I had made an appointment to meet with her. Despite the fact I'm a medium, it's often difficult to do your own reading—especially on subjects where you are way too close to the situation. I was interested to see whether my sister was reaching out.

Emelia was already at the store when I arrived that morning. I put down my things and poked my head into the Zen Den to see if she was ready for me.

"Is it about CJ?" she asked.

"Why, yes!" I said. I wasn't particularly surprised she knew; she *is* a psychic after all.

"That's good. Because she's been bugging me all morning!"

Spirits don't experience time in the same way we do in the 3D world. Obviously, my thinking about my sister had called her closer. I sat down, and we prepared ourselves to connect to the spirit realm.

I reached out to CJ and asked how she was doing. The medium said she was very confused. CJ couldn't figure out why she had died.

Yup. That was my sis. She never did grasp how truly sick she was. Being disconnected like that meant she never made choices that would support her general health and healing. Other than wondering why she had died, she seemed pretty good. In later visits some deep regrets surfaced, and I tried to help her work through some of those.

Recently she said she had been working on our behalf and helped avoid a "close call." I hadn't had any close calls driving but realized it might be a future event or be in reference to her husband. I checked in with him and, sure enough, about two weeks prior, while driving, he had drifted out of his lane and only at the last moment corrected his course and avoided a head-on collision. Within forty-eight hours, I too had a close call pulling out into traffic. Whew! Thank you, CJ!

Two Angels Come to Call

A friend called and asked if I could meet her at the store and do a reading for her. There was someone from her past that had been screaming at her for months for a meeting. She wanted me to come in and see if we could make a connection. She didn't tell me much more, and I didn't ask. Too much information can cloud my perception.

As I made my way into meet her, I began seeing images. I had a sense of a person tumbling down something like Alice's Wonderland rabbit hole. I suspected I had already begun to tap into the situation.

Once at the store, I cleared the space and created a sacred area. I grabbed some Botswana agates for our pockets. It is a perfect crystal to help shamanic work in the lower realms. It can help make you invisible to the low frequency entities while you move about in that realm to do your work.

Prayers were said, and we stated our intention. I lit a candle to signal we were about to start, to light our way and to show us the way back.

I asked her if I could hold her hands for a few moments. As soon as I did, I recognized that the images that I had seen on my trip in were indeed related to this reading.

In the vision this person was tumbling, endlessly twisting and flipping, over and over. I couldn't tell if it was a male or a female, and it turns out her friend was androgynous. There was quite a bit of fear and flailing of arms and legs. It wasn't a pleasant image. I related this to the client, and she confirmed that, yes, that was a sense that she was getting also. I was picking up some heavy drug use, and she also confirmed that. It turned out that we were connecting to the spirit of her best friend, Mikey, who had passed away sixteen years ago.

Mikey seemed to be reaching out in desperation for some help to quit tumbling through this dark hole. He was ready to move into the light.

On his birthday sixteen years ago, she was preparing for a party later in the day. She was busy, and Mikey (a roommate at the time) was getting ready to leave the house and run some errands with a friend. As usual, he wanted to give her a big hug, and she brushed him off and said, "I'm too busy. I'll see you in a few hours, so run along." Of course, he was not going to return. As you can imagine, this missed opportunity had been something haunting her for almost two decades.

Mikey had joined up with a friend that day. They had parked next to railroad tracks and gotten high. Mikey got out of the car and crossed the tracks to use the bathroom away from his friend. His friend in the car looked down at his phone and was startled by a thump on the windshield. To his horror, it was Mikey's shoe with his foot still in it. Mikey had just been hit by a train. Awful.

We had enough validation that we were connecting with Mikey, so I asked him if he wanted some help to quit tumbling down the black hole. Of course he did. It turns out that, in life, Christina had been his rock and had provided stability. He was reaching out to her once again for that stability in his death.

I told him we would not come down to get him, but he could choose to come up to us. I instructed Christina to hold my right hand across the table and stretch out our other hand so he could join us in a three-way hold. I invited him to reach out to grab our hands.

It took a few seconds, but we both felt that he did reach up and grab our hands. At this point I saw him holding onto our hands. He hadn't stabilized yet, like someone being swept away in a strong wind tunnel. He was hanging on for dear life in order to not be sucked back into the black hole.

As a little time passed, I sensed he was becoming more stable, and instead of being sucked back into the hole, he seemed to have been able to put his feet down and was standing next to us, holding our hands.

While we talked, Mikey held up his index finger to show me tape wrapped around it. I shared that with Christina. She started to cry-laugh, so I knew that we had hit on a validation point.

She shared that he was something of a MacGyver type, and that he always had black electrical tape with him. Once he had fallen off

149

his skateboard and really tore up the tip of his index finger. He had used black electrical tape to tape it back in place for it to heal. Another validation that we indeed were speaking with Mikey.

I asked if Christina had any questions for him. He answered the question she had tortured herself over for almost twenty years—was he upset about her not giving him a hug before he left that day? No! He was upset that he had been so careless and gotten so involved in the drugs that he lost his physical life. That's what he was sad about. He was upset that he had been tumbling out of control down this hole since his death and was ready to stabilize and to move on. But he needed her help. Just like in life, he was reaching out to his bestie to help him get stable and move on.

I then did a dimensional jump with her and Mikey to rewrite his last day slightly.

While we can't change the outcome of the day or how he passed away, we can rewrite parts of it and bring them into a higher frequency quite easily.

I had her close her eyes and go back to the moment when he was about to leave the house that morning. This time, rather than walking out the door without the hug, I switched it up slightly. In this new timeline, she was still rebuffing him, but he playfully grabbed her, gave her a big hug, and planted smooches on her cheek. She was both annoyed and amused and then sent him off so that she could get ready for his party. This gave her a new dialogue to remember about her role that morning. The hug had happened. That was complete.

She had also been laboring under the false narrative that she could have saved him. Mikey was quite clear in his message to her today that she could not have saved him. It was not her responsibility. He was not upset with her in any way about how it turned out.

About that time I noticed that his spirit had changed again. This time he felt stable, and he was glowing.

I sensed that this was the perfect time to help him move on. I asked her and Mikey if they had anything else they wanted to talk to each other about before I asked the angels to open the door.

They said their goodbyes, and I asked for the angels to come in and open the portal for Mikey to be able to move into the light.

Interestingly, just about this time, someone came into the store and heard the clerk on duty greeting them. I didn't think much about it at the time. I'll get back to that encounter later!

I announced that Mikey was ready and called on Archangel Michael, Archangel Azrael, or whomever would be most appropriate to come and help us move him into the light. I humbly asked that they open the door and show Mikey the path into the light. They did.

Then something happened I had never seen before. The two angels picked him up underneath his arms and literally flew him over to the entrance and deposited him in front of the door. They said, "We can bring you this far, but it's up to you whether or not you walk through."

I also had the sense that a number of his ancestors showed up at that moment. In particular I was picking up a grandmother vibe and mentioned it. She confirmed that she, too, was sensing her.

I asked again if she was ready to say goodbye and checked in with Mikey to see if there was anything left to be said. They gave each other the equivalent of a spiritual hug, and Mikey turned and walked through the door. I watched as he faded into the light.

Humorously, I saw this grandmother spirit that had come to greet him literally swatting him on his behind, kind of pushing him along into the light tunnel. It was rather amusing. I did share that with the client, who knew them both and confirmed the grandmother was Portuguese with quite a spunk about her. She could also see her swatting him in the rear end, getting him to move along quickly!

We continued to talk, and she shared with me that, three years after his passing, she had gone back to check on the cross that they had placed as a marker at his death spot. She brought along a man that she was about to marry who turned out not to be the best choice.

While they were there, she crossed the railroad track and somehow got her foot stuck and fell. They both heard a train whistle in the distance, and panic set in. She managed to get herself up and off the track. She looked around, but as you have probably already imagined, there was no train anywhere to be seen.

I reminded her that, during the session, she had asked what happened and how in the world had he not seen the train and been hit by it.

She shared she thought that episode had always been Mikey trying to warn her about this man. I think it was Mikey showing her what had happened to him. He was in a disoriented drug high and gotten his foot caught. He just couldn't free himself in time, and it turned out to be his demise.

As we were closing down the session, the angels instructed me to close the portal that Mikey had been falling down for so many years. I used the imagery of a submarine hatch. I closed the hatch and securely locked it by turning the big wheel and then welded it shut around the entrance with unconditional God Love so that nothing could come or go through it any longer.

We closed the session, cut our cords, and I sent her on her way.

Mikey did contact me within about ten minutes with one final message for his friend. Beyond the fact that he was grateful and doing just fine, he was very thankful for her help in moving past this. He also wanted her to get the message that she needed to take care of her body. It was important, and he was regretful he hadn't taken better care of his own.

After the client left, I found out that the two people who had come into the store earlier turned out to be a deaf couple. Our clerk, Jonathan, encouraged them to write down what they wanted, but they refused.

We're friendly with our customers, but Jonathan doesn't really like to give or get hugs.

He shared with me that they each hugged him when they first came into the store, and he was ok with the hugging. Despite the fact that they couldn't communicate in the conventional ways, he understood them completely and felt great love from them.

They made their selection and stepped to the pay station. The customers each hugged Jonathan again, and the man signed, "You are beautiful." Jonathan does not understand American Sign Language. Not a single sign. But he was clear what the man said to him.

They paid with cash, and Jonathan looked down to get the register receipt. When he looked up, they were gone!

He hurried to the door to see how that would even be possible, but there was no one around.

There is no way they could have gotten out the door and disappeared in the time it would have taken him to look down to get the receipt and look back up.

Even before knowing what had been going on in our session, Jonathan was convinced that he had just encountered two angels. I have to concur.

Oh, and the necklace they selected? One of the crystals I personally dug and wrapped.

What a privilege to have angels visit us. What an honor that they selected one of my blessed crystal necklaces.

I don't think they were deaf. I think when angels speak, it's hard for human ears to hear and understand. I'm pretty sure they speak light language and use soul words.

They paid cash and wouldn't write anything down so there would be no physical evidence of their visit. Clever. Always leaving it up to us to interpret and choose faith or not.

What a validation that, when you call on angels, they come. I have been weepy ever since, a regular symbol to me that I have been in the presence of the Divine. So thank you to the angels for coming and being a part of this healing. We are deeply grateful.

Books Fly

It's important to remember when you work with spirits and spirit guides that they usually speak in symbols and metaphors. The challenge is to understand the message.

On this particular Monday, Jonathan \and one of our mediums were at the store before opening. They were still back in the break area when my husband, Robert, came in to do a project. Robert walked into the store and flipped on the lights to find that there were four books on the floor. They were *Illusions* by Richard Bach. That book was absolutely one of the most life-changing books in my life. It was the book that set me on this life course. I saw the selection of this book as a clear message: somebody was trying to reach out to me.

Books fall out of the bookshelf sometimes, so I wanted to try and debunk it first. I checked with Jonathan, and no, they hadn't been facing out and then fallen over. They were placed with the spine facing out.

I was on the phone with them, hearing about the situation as they put the books back on the shelf. One of the things that our medium noticed was the one that was separated from the other three looked as if the spine had been mangled. She picked that one up and took it to the Zen Den to do a little meditating and clearing on it.

Robert was observing as Jonathan replaced the remaining three books on the shelf with spine facing out on the bookshelf. Our medium, Jonathan, and Robert were looking at the newly replaced books when all three remaining books—literally, not figuratively—flew out off of the bookshelf and landed on the floor again!

Now, my husband, who was raised in the Catholic tradition, muttered, "Well, that was interesting," as he turned around and headed quickly to the front of the store.

Guess it was a bit too much that early in the day for him. No kidding! Clearly something was trying to get our attention. We have weird stuff happen at the store all the time, but we don't often have this level of weird.

It's unusual for things to go flying off the bookshelf. It's more unusual for it to have been witnessed by three people. So the question was, what was going on?

We all immediately jumped to "Oh, it's something bad; it's something negative. It's a demon." Well, no, it's not always something negative. It was a good lesson to not jump to conclusions.

We did all kinds of holy water and smudging and cleaning, but the space still felt unsettled. I arrived at the store and tried to ascertain what was happening. When I got there, I felt unsettled emotionally and energetically. I tried to settle down, but it wasn't working.

Later in the day, I was inspired to check in with one of my most trusted guides, Sabrina. She tapped in and confirmed that there was an entity in the store, and it had become trapped. It thought

158

it could use one of the portals we've got in the store. We've got that portal locked down, and nothing can come in or go out of it without permission. Seems it was angry about being trapped.

Sabrina and I discovered that this entity had come in because it was curious about all the high energy in the store. As a result of being trapped, it was thrashing around, trying to find a way out.

When we tapped in, we found it was clearly intelligent. It had picked the book *Illusions*, reaching out to me. I alone had the authority in that space to open up a way for this entity to leave.

Working remotely, Sabrina had me place a crystal that we could both focus on, giving us a physical and energetic connection. We tapped into that crystal energetically and allowed the crystal to open a portal and help this entity find its way out of the store safely and properly. I called in Archangel Michael for the entity, and I introduced them, saying, "Archangel Michael is here to help you."

Sabrina reminded me that not everything is evil just because we don't understand it. This was an intelligent entity, and it knew how to reach out by throwing these books on the floor.

It's a good lesson. I wasn't really afraid, but I did feel unsettled. I liken it to working with a wild animal that's beautiful and powerful, but it doesn't belong in your store. It is not evil. It doesn't want to be there any more than you want it there.

By listening to and respecting it, we were able communicate. Once it knew I had the authority and wanted to help it get out of the store, it calmed down. Its objective was to get my attention and get it out of there. So that's what we did.

Once I opened up a portal for it to leave, it left safely and properly, and it was able to return to where it was from.

The moral of this story: before you jump to conclusions, get quiet and tap into the situation. Obviously protect yourself, and, if needed, ask for a trusted spiritual guide. But not everything is automatically evil. Sometimes it just needs someone in authority to show it the way out.

No, You're Not Crazy

By now, I hope you've seen glimpses of your own story in mine. It is my desire for you to know at the core of your being that you are not crazy when you are experiencing these types of phenomena. You're different, yes. And while that might create tension in your life and relationships, it can also open doors for you that you might never have discovered had you not opened yourself to these new possibilities.

If my story has inspired you to find your own voice, then read on for some methods that I've used and might work for you. Like any recipe, try it, but then mix up the ingredients and make it your own.

Getting Started on Your Own Journey

What do you need to get started? It's simple. A desire to know more. A willingness to question and test the information you uncover. Courage to evaluate the data and make your own decisions. A conviction to live the truth you find. And most importantly, an open mind to explore new possibilities you uncover.

The following chapters will offer some detailed information and instructions on how to facilitate your own awakening. It will help you connect with and communicate directly with the angelic realm and meet your guardian angels. Be bold! But be cautious. As in any trip you plan to take into a new, unfamiliar place, be prepared. Use your discernment. Plan ahead. Consult with others who have already made the journey. Be prepared for the unexpected.

Ready? Great. Let's start with your plan.

Take some time to decide what it is you want to accomplish with this new venture. Do you want to explore gifts you've kept suppressed all your life? Maybe you want to find a way to develop a closer relationship with the Divine and angels. No matter your goal, the first thing I recommend is to create a sacred space for your work.

Preparing Your Sacred Space

Creating a sacred space for prayer or meditation can be as simple as carving out a spot in the corner of your room or designating a favorite chair as your spot. First, physically clean the area. Next, you'll want to clear any stale or negative energy. This helps raise the frequencies, making it easier to meditate and connect with the angelic realm. There are a number of ways to accomplish this also. I love using sacred herbs like sage or lavender to smudge before I settle into a meditation session. Burning incense is also a great way to start.

Why Clear Stale Energy?

Clearing negative or stale energy brings the frequencies of your surroundings to a higher level and creates a sacred space, promoting a more calm, balanced, and healthy environment. Plus it just feels better.

Every living thing leaves a plume of energy as it moves through life. Science has discovered we humans can be identified by our individual bioplume. Each one of us is unique, and our plume contains our personal microviruses, microbacteria, sweat, sound (frequencies), and heat. When we—and those around us—are healthy and happy, we leave less stale energy that needs to be cleared. When we are surrounded by stale, negative, chaotic, or dis-eased energy, we can be affected by those subtle frequencies in a negative way.

Residual Energy

We can be affected by the residual energy around us. If that energy is overtly negative, we will start to resonate with those lower frequencies. Here's an example of residual energy.

Imagine a mirror. Touch it and you will leave your fingerprints on the surface. Even if you wipe the fingerprints off, you will still see the heat energy signature of your fingers on the mirror if you use a thermal camera. Though you might not see the fingerprints, you've left some of your energy on the mirror.

After a period of time, that heat signature will fade. Handle the mirror a lot, and you will have a lot of fingerprints and a lot of heat signatures on the mirror. If the energy on your hands was dirty (as in, you were sick) you can expect to find viruses or bacteria and potentially hotter fingerprints left behind.

Taking the mirror analogy further, let's say you come home from a long day at work or school and plop down on your favorite chair or sofa. You are leaving energy signatures everywhere and on everything. Sad energy, mad energy, sick energy, happy energy—it all gets left behind on everything and anything you touch.

Then let's say you wanted to use your mirror, but it had a lot of fingerprints (energy signatures) all over it. You would clean it off to get a better reflection. That's exactly want you are doing when you clear your space using smudging or a technique with frequencies or vibrations.

What Is Smudging?

Smudging is a ceremony or procedure to remove negative or stale energy or influences from a person, place, or object. It is also an effective method for energizing or blessing a person, place, or object. It has been used for centuries by many different cultures to create sacred spaces.

Many know of the Native American traditions using smudge. There are many resources that focus on the cultural and religious traditions. I'll cover some simple step-by-step instructions to clear negative or stale energy and create a loving, sacred environment in your home or office. You may choose to make it a spiritual occasion—or not.

First, gather your tools such as smudge, incense, clearing spray, a feather or fanning tool, a shell or ashtray to catch ashes. You can also add essential oils, crystals, and or any protection items you choose. You may choose to line your shell or ashtray with salt or sand for added protection.

Bundles of herbs for smudging can be readily acquired in metaphysical stores or online. They can come loose or in bundles small, medium, or large. Even a small bundle will normally do a good job for a medium-sized area. You can reuse the bundle if you don't burn it all.

Next, do a physical cleaning. Stale and negative energy can get stuck or hide in clutter. Open windows, and air the place out. Visualize bringing in fresh, clean energy, bright and cheerful. Turn on the fan to facilitate moving the old out and bringing in the fresh.

Herbs to Use in Smudging

White sage is universally useful for healing and blessing a person, place, or object. It is great for clearing stale energy and unwanted influences around you and creating a sacred space.

Cedar is a known for protection and is great to cleanse a home or apartment when first moving in, inviting unwanted spirits to leave, and protecting a person, place, or object from unwanted influences.

Sweetgrass or Seneca grass (also called holy grass,) and vanilla grass (which has a sweet, vanilla-like scent,) are helpful in bringing the essence of the feminine and the blessing of Mother Earth's love. It also reminds us that the earth provides everything we need.

Lavender is often used to remove negative energy and protect against evil. It calms and harmonizes the mind, restores emotional balance, and can create a peaceful harmonious environment. It also attracts angelic beings. Burning loose lavender is best done on charcoal tablets.

Copal is sacred tree sap from Mexico and is similar to frankincense. It produces a scent that is crisp, clean, sharp, and somewhat citrus-like. Burning copal is best done on charcoal tablets.

Frankincense is a tree resin that can be used to cleanse and protect the soul. Frankincense is important to most major religions in the world and is still found in many of their rituals. Folklore claims that it helps to ease depression and promote clairvoyance. Burning frankincense is best done on charcoal tablets.

Myrrh is a tree resin and is said to help one maintain a state of enlightenment. It also helps you see your own truth. Burning myrrh is best done on charcoal tablets.

Crystals

You may choose to add healing or protective crystals to your clearing techniques and ceremonies. The frequencies of the different crystals can help strengthen your aura, keep you focused, and help raise the vibrations in the space you are clearing. They are *not* required and are completely optional, so don't worry if you don't have any crystals. If you do want to use crystals, they will be more effective if they have been cleared, charged, and programmed. It is simple to do and recommended if you plan on using them during the ceremony.

How to Clear, Charge, and Program Crystals

Clearing: one tried-and-true way to clear crystals is with salt water. Get a container you will not be using later for food and throw in a handful of salt. Any table salt will work. I often get questions from clients if they should use Himalayan pink salt. You can, but plain old, cheap salt will do the trick. Salt has green prana. It's the frequency of green, and that salt is a desiccant, pulling the negativity from the crystals.

Fill the bowl with enough water to completely cover the crystals. Soak them for at least thirty minutes. Rinse them in clear water to remove all traces of the salt. Rub gently if appropriate, and envision any dirty energy being lifted off and properly disposed of. Pat them dry.

Caution: not all gemstones can tolerate salt water. Check before soaking them.

You can also smudge your crystals. Light your smudge and waft the smoke around your crystals to clear them.

To charge your crystal, you can hold it as you pray over it. Or set it out in bright sun, an electrical storm, full moon, or bury it overnight. You will definitely want to mark where you bury it, as more than one crystal has been lost this way!

To program your crystal, hold it and focus your attention on the crystal. Say, "Crystal, listen to me. Strengthen my aura and protect me from psychic contamination." Use whatever simple command you wish your crystal to do for you. If you want all your crystals to do the same thing, you can program them together. If not, work on programming each one individually.

There you go. Your crystals are now cleared, charged, programmed, and ready to help you in your ceremony. You can either use them in your space or hold them while you conduct your smudging.

Here are a few crystals to consider.

Obsidian is a powerful protection crystal. It helps clear, strengthen, and protect your aura. It is very strong protection against psychic attacks. Obsidian has a lot of earth energy. It's easily programmed to form a barrier of protection to prevent unwanted energies from entering your space or your aura. Place it in your sacred space, and program it to form a protective shield that prevents anything evil from entering. It's self-cleaning, which is great for setting it and forgetting it!

Black tourmaline is very grounding and one of the most powerful stones for psychic protection and shielding against negative energy.

Rose quartz is known as the stone of love and can help keep your heart chakra open while being protected. It can help you stay loving and prevent you from becoming bitter.

Amethyst is an excellent choice to connect to the Divine, protect your aura and shield you against negativity. It's a master stone and a must for any collection.

Any of your favorite crystals or talismans can be cleared and programmed to shield you during smudging and during meditation.

Now, Light the Sage or Incense

Now that you have your smudging tools ready, your crystals placed (optional), and you and your space are clean, you can begin the smudging ceremony. Say a prayer over the items and thank them for helping you clear the stale energy and for creating a sacred space. Light your bundle of sage, smudge, or incense, and allow it to burn for a moment and then extinguish the flame so it begins to smoke. The smoke is what you will be wafting through your space.

Place the smoking bundle with the lit end down in the receptacle with the fireproof sand or salt to catch the ashes. Holding the shell (or ashtray) in one hand and feather in the other, pick a starting point and begin at the bottom right of your designated space. Use caution. There is a hot ember that can start a fire.

You can go clockwise to bring in energy, counterclockwise to get it to leave. As you move through your space, have the intention of filling it with white light, love, and joy. Any of the low vibrations like anger, hate, and despair aren't compatible and can't coexist with the higher vibration of love. Your job is to bring the vibrations of your space up to something closer to love.

Here is an example of a statement you may choose to use:

"This is a place of light and love. All who enter are transformed by the power of unconditional God Love!"

Using the feather to ceremoniously waft smoke into the corners of the space, clear your chair, pillows, candles, and anything else you will be using during your meditation. I often smudge myself by carefully wafting the incense smoke around my aura. Imagine all the stale energy being cleared and replaced with light and love.

If I'm doing this at the start of my meditation, I usually only spend a moment or so. If you need to smudge the entire area or whole house, then separate those events from your meditation time.

The first time smudging, or if you haven't smudged for a long time, will likely take about an hour or so. I keep my house pretty clear energetically, so these quickies are what I call a "spot clearing."

Using Clearing Sprays

If burning incense or smudge is not practical, you can use a clearing spray. Follow the same steps as if you were going to burn a smudge stick or incense but use a clearing spray instead. A feather or fan is helpful to waft the spray into the corners in the same way you would use it with smoke.

There are a number of clearing sprays available at stores or online. If you would like to create your own, here are a few recipes I created for a two-oz spray bottle.

Recipe one (my favorite):
      Four drops lavender essential oil
      Pinch of salt
      Fill with (cheapest) vodka
      Shake and use as needed

Recipe two:

> Thirty drops sage essential oil
> Four drops frankincense essential oil
> Pinch of salt
> Fill with holy or blessed water
> Shake and use as needed

Why use vodka? First, it doesn't have a smell, and if I use it to clear energy from my hands, it doesn't dry them out. I will also use it to clear furniture and my bed, and it evaporates quickly and doesn't stain.

Holy water can be purchased from your local Catholic gift store or church, or you can make your own.

A quick Google search will provide you with complete instructions on how to follow Catholic procedures or inspire you on how to create your own ritual to bless the water.

Clearing Your Space with Frequencies

If you have tuning forks, use them. Most don't, so no problem. Download the high sacred solfeggio frequency of 963 hertz to your phone. Clapping loudly also works. Grab some pots and pans and a wooden spoon and move through the space making noise. Reclaim your space with statements of authority. An example of what I use is "this is a space of light and love! Only those from the highest source for my highest good may enter." Act like you mean it! Use your most authoritative voice.

All the noise and clapping will break up stale energy. Your positive intentions along with praying brings in happy, upbeat frequencies.

Have the intention of filling the space with light and love.

No, you don't have to do this every time you want to meditate. How often do you need to do it? Well, it's like dusting your furniture. You just know when it's time.

Shielding Your Sacred Space from Negative People and Energy

If you have problems with negative energy or people entering your sacred area, you can further protect your space with a thin line of salt along the threshold of the area. Putting salt, crystals, holy water, or essential oils at the entrance of the room or area is also highly effective in keeping negative energy outside of your sacred spaces.

Obsidian at the thresholds is effective in keeping unwanted things from entering your space. Obsidian is also one of the crystals that releases any stale or negative energy safely and doesn't require clearing on your part. Refer to the section on how to clear, charge, and program your crystal if you plan on using obsidian.

I have obsidian at all my doorways, one on either side of the doorjamb at home and at the store. I have them programmed to form a grid so that anything overtly negative or outright evil cannot come through without being invited.

Sometimes it's uncomfortable and a little unsettling when I have someone who comes to the store door, stops, takes a quick look around, and then leaves. I know that my obsidian is working. When I look at this person, I realize that their vibrations don't match up with what I'm doing and the high vibrations at the Rock Shop.

Once, I was distracted talking and joking around with some regular customers and not paying attention. There was a man that had come into the entrance of the store but stopped at the interior door where the obsidian was placed. He stood there for several moments. Without thinking about it, I said to the man, "Well, come on in."

I immediately knew that I had committed an error! He stepped in the door, and the first thing out of his mouth was, "You really have to be careful about vampires around here now."

The regular customers and I all looked at each other and realized I had invited him in! My friends and customers in the store at the time happened to be quite familiar with light work, and we were trying to get this guy and his energy out as quickly as possible. After he left, we immediately set about smudging the place, clearing, and blessing. And yes, we were singing and clapping and dancing and making declarations.

Believe me, if you have an effective grid, evil can't get in unless you invite it in.

Essential Oils for Dispersing Negativity and Creating Your Sacred Space

Essential oils have been used for hundreds of years in countless cultures to help disperse negativity and create sacred spaces. Here are just a few of the oils you could use to help you clear yourself or your space of negative or stale energy. You have the option of using them in a spray, in a diffuser, or anointing yourself, another person, or an object.

Be certain to properly dilute any essential oil before applying it to your skin. You will need some sort of a fatty carrier oil. Even olive oil will serve as a carrier oil in a pinch. Follow the instructions on the label, but you generally don't want a solution stronger than about 10 percent if you are applying it to your skin. Use full strength in a diffuser or if you are anointing something other than a person. You can put a drop or two on your palm, gently rub your hands together once or twice to activate the oil (don't rub too vigorously, a few quick rubs will do the trick). Drag your hands through your aura to clear it and balance your chakras. Take a deep breath of the fragrant oil. Then ceremoniously anoint yourself by rubbing your shoulders or the crown of your head before sitting down to meditate.

See the earlier recipes for creating a spray. If you are using the oils on your skin or another person, please follow any instructions on the bottle and use caution if you are pregnant or have any health concerns.

Here are some of my favorites and how they may help you with clearing ceremonies:

Basil—aura cleansing, purification.

Bay—spiritual cleansing, purification.

Cajeput—purification, cleansing, protection, dispels negative energies.

Cedarwood, Virginian—protection and purification.

Citronella—purification, dispelling negative energy.

Clary sage—protection and psychic clarity.

Eucalyptus—purification, exorcism, banishing negative energies.

Frankincense—Anointing, psychic protection, purification, dispelling of negative and harmful energies, create and purify sacred spaces, exorcism.

Galbanum—purification, protection, banishing negative energies.

Geranium—protection, dispelling apprehension and negativity.

Grapefruit—to help deal with jealousy, envy, bitterness.

Hyssop—purification, protection, spiritual/aura cleansing.

Lavender—inner peace and purification.

Lemongrass—purification, to clear psychic channels.

Lemon verbena—purification, cleansing of items.

Lime—protection, energy of action, purification.

Juniper—purification, protection, to dispel negative energies and entities.

Myrrh—psychic protection, purification, dispelling of negative and harmful energies.

Niaouli—Purification, protection, release of negative energies that "clog up" the physical and mental bodies, aura cleansing.

Peppermint—purification and dispels negative thought forms.

Pine—purification, dispels negative energy, crystal cleansing, protection.

Sage—aura cleansing, dispels negative energies, purification, protection.

Sandalwood—dispels fears and negative energies.

Tea tree—aura cleansing, protection, purification.

Thyme, white—purification, protection, inner strength, and emotional courage.

Vetiver—protection, grounding.

Cautions When Smudging and Clearing Energy

Beyond the obvious cautions when using fire and burning objects, be careful if you have, or suspect you have, "uninvited guests" that are reluctant to leave your space. Provoking negative spirits will not normally have a positive outcome from your efforts to clear them. You're likely to have better results by filling the area with light and love than banishing and expelling. Low-frequency entities are not comfortable in high-frequency spaces. They will leave on their own.

Most importantly, you do *not* have the authority to send something or someone to "hell," or whatever you may call it in your tradition. That will backfire on you. Don't do it! You *can* send something or someone back to source or back to where it is from and love it back into perfection. Trust me—that is a *much* better choice.

Meditation

As you start your journey, one of the most powerful tools at your disposal is meditation. I covered the subject earlier in the book, providing the proof that you *can* meditate. It's a skill set you can develop. If you are having trouble quieting your mind, then you've got an out-of-control toddler brain running your show. Chances are that's not working out so well for you. Don't worry, you *can* turn your life around and bring more love, joy, health, and prosperity into your world. Mediation is a surefire way to make positive changes.

Some Quick Tips before You Get started—Breathwork Exercise

One perfect way to learn how to quiet your toddler brain is with a breathwork exercise. It's simple to do. Imagine a figure eight laying on its side like the infinity sign. At first, you might draw it out on a piece of paper if it helps you imagine it. Next, use your finger and trace around the lines as you slowly breathe. This exercise if perfect in teaching children.

Start in the center of the figure eight. Breathe in to a slow count of four, tracing with your finger along the top right curve of the figure eight. When you reach the furthest point on the right side, exhale to the count of four and trace the bottom of the curve until your finger returns to the center of the symbol. Repeat this for the other side of the image. Inhale to the count of four to get to the other side, and exhale to the count of four to come back to the center.

Breathe slowly. Take your time. After a few times, you don't need to use your finger. Just visualize it in your mind's eye. See this figure eight, and really concentrate on it.

Breathing like this is not natural, which forces you to concentrate on your physical body. As a result, your toddler brain's like, "Hey, what's going on? I'm not going to sit here; this is stupid. Let's get back to my stories." You've really got to negotiate and teach your brain how to be quiet. This is something to occupy your two-year-old toddler brain while you start to get things under control. Do that exercise a couple of times throughout the day or as you sit down to pray or meditate.

There are any number of breathwork exercises you can use. A quick YouTube or Google search will net many examples. Find one, or some, that work for you. Any breathwork that forces you to pay attention to what's going on physically is an excellent way to distract your toddler brain and help train your body to stay in the present moment.

Next, create a situation where you're not going to be interrupted. Look, it's a busy, noisy world. If you've got family or pets or neighbors, then you may get interrupted. But at least in the beginning, work on having the space and the time of at least five or ten uninterrupted minutes.

I created a designated spot where I do my meditations. If you can carve out a corner of a room or a special chair, that's great. I just covered how to create your sacred space, but don't let it stop you if that's not an option.

As I start my meditations, I like to light a candle. This may or may not be appropriate for you. Electronic candles are great option if you can't light a flame where you live. Or you can omit using a candle all together.

I use either smudge or incense before I begin to prepare my space and bring the frequencies up. I have an altar table with a beautiful bowl of crystals, my candle, my abalone shell, feather-fan, a stick of white sage, and a stick of incense. I have a lovely pinch pot to catch the spent match.

As I get started, I light the candle and declare my intentions. "I light this candle to signify I am beginning this meditation session. Any and all who come, come from the highest source, for my highest good and the highest good of all."

Then I state, "I allow this flame to be the symbol of light and love and ask it to illuminate my path, and it allows my angels and my guides to see where I am."

I then use one of my favorite prayers. One is the Lord's Prayer; the other is the Prayer of Protection.

The Lord's Prayer from the King James Version of the Bible:

> Our Father which art in heaven,
> Hallowed be thy name.
> Thy kingdom come, Thy will be done in earth, as it is in heaven.

181

Give us this day our daily bread.
And forgive us our debts, as we forgive
our debtors.
And lead us not into temptation but
deliver us from evil: For thine is the
kingdom, and the power, and the glory,
forever. Amen.

The Prayer of Protection by James Dillet Freeman:
The Light of God surrounds me.
The Love of God enfolds me.
The Power of God protects me.
The Presence of God watches over me.
Wherever I am, God is!

Here's a suggestion from one of my candle vendors, Crystal Journey Candles, that I use a lot: "May I open my mind to receive wisdom from higher powers. Allow their guidance to lead me to peace and tranquility all the days of my life."

Those are some of my choices. Find a statement and ceremony that resonates with you.

After you light a candle, make your prayer statement, and clear the space if needed. You can set a timer for ten or fifteen minutes if you need to mind your time.

Get comfortable in a position you can maintain with minimal shifting duration of your session. Choose a spot where you're not going to be interrupted. I like to sit on some floor pillows with my back against a recliner in the space to support my back. The pillows elevate me a little, and the chair supports me so I'm more comfortable than sitting without it. I sit cross-legged and prefer to take my shoes off but find whatever's comfortable for you. You can lay down if you like, but if you're just getting started, laying down may put you to sleep, which isn't all bad. Obviously, it's a great way to fall asleep. But if you're just learning to quiet your toddler brain through meditation, try to stay awake.

You can choose to turn on some background noise. I have a sound machine, and I play a babbling brook sound to focus on. The white noise from a fan or air conditioner is also a great focal point.

Once you get quiet, the first thing that will likely happen is you'll be distracted. You're not used to doing this, so be prepared—your toddler brain is going to fight back when you quit focusing exclusively on its stories. A distracting thought will likely pop up. Focus on your breathing until whatever thought has passed.

You can use the image of a beautiful little box that you open and put your thoughts or your worries in and close the lid. Imagine putting it outside the door. I tell myself, "I can always retrieve it from the box later, but for right now, I'm going to leave it in the box."

Another way you can deal with distracting thoughts is to imagine a beautiful babbling brook beside you. There are some leaves, and you just put that thought or worry on a leaf, set it on the babbling brook, and let it float away.

A third way to do it would be to see a whiteboard or a chalkboard. You can see there's all kinds of things written on it, and you erase everything until the whiteboard is blank. And then, if something pops up or shows up on the whiteboard, you erase it away again.

There are a couple of solid ways that you can learn how to meditate in the beginning. Get quiet, acknowledge that you've got a little out-of-control two-year-old toddler brain. Frankly, if you don't get it under control, it's going to continue to run your life, and you're going to think that you *are* your thoughts. That may not be working out so good for you.

With practice you will learn to dodge those self-destructive thoughts that come your way and simply observe them as they pass you by. This is really a valuable skill to regain control of your life and bring all the wonder, joy, prosperity, health, and love you desire into your life.

Do you need to meditate every day? No. But the more you meditate, the faster you will journey inward, and the faster you will grow spiritually. When you stop letting the fear of what you will find when you look deep into yourself stop you, you will be amazed at the wonderous person you find.

I always have my journal next to me while I meditate. I often communicate with spirit in this quiet state, and they channel information or messages, which I want to record.

If you want to connect with the angelic realm, raise your frequencies by raising your emotions. Writing in a gratitude journal will help break the cycle of negative thinking in your life.

I'm Feeling Overwhelmed and Unsure How to Proceed

It's completely normal to feel a bit overwhelmed in the beginning of your spiritual journey. Deep breath! Let's figure it out together. Take a break and go get some paper and a pen or pencil you love to use. Better yet, get your journal. If you don't have a journal, create one. A simple spiral bound notebook will work just fine. It doesn't have to be fancy.

The Benefits of Journaling

My aim is to put down on paper what I see and what I feel in the best *and simplest way.*
—Ernest Hemingway

Journaling allows people to clarify their thoughts and feelings, thereby gaining valuable self-knowledge. It's also a good problem-solving tool. Oftentimes, one can hash out a problem and come up with solutions more easily on paper. Journaling about traumatic events helps one process them by fully exploring and releasing the emotions involved and by engaging both hemispheres of the brain in the process, allowing the experience to become fully integrated within one's mind.

Journaling can clarify which areas of your life would benefit from self-reflection. It can also serve as record of your life experiences. This will help you understand more about yourself and your gifts. Once you are more comfortable with yourself, it's easier to navigate tricky relationships with friends, family, and coworkers. Journaling is also a great way to record any messages you receive from angels, spirit guides and ancestors. In other words. You need a journal!

Get Started with a Gratitude Journal

If you are stuck in a pattern of negative thinking or self-talk that's keeping you in a cycle of low-frequency emotions and situations that needs to be upgraded, a gratitude journal is a great way to begin to break that destructive habit and get you and your life turned around. If your immediate reaction to this suggestion is "There's nothing to be grateful for in my life..." or "I'm not negative, I'm being realistic," I'm sorry to say, you're got a negative attitude. You may not see yourself as a negative person. It can be a very subtle underpinning of your worldview of others and yourself. Negativity is extremely toxic, and if you want to achieve any level of enlightenment and work closely with the angelic realm, then it's imperative you change that negativity around to positivity.

The emotion of negativity is one of the lower emotions and thus has a frequency that resonates with and can attract the lower entities and experiences to your life. Remember the radio station example? If you constantly tune into the negativity station, that's the playlist you will have in your experience. High-level wellness and supreme joy is difficult to achieve when you are in low emotional states.

If you desire to communicate with angels and your spirit guides, it's important to create a space for them to come to you. It's critical to bring the frequency up, in you and the space around you.

Gratitude Journal Exercise

Obtain a journal and label it or a section of it "Gratitude."

Make a commitment that, for a minimum of twenty-one days, you will create a journal entry with at least one thing you are grateful for that day. Experts tell us it takes at least twenty-one days for a new habit to take hold. If you can't muster twenty-one days, pick the number of days you are willing to commit to.

Pick a time of the day to make your entries. Right before you go to bed is an excellent time. It sets the tone for your sleep and sends you off to your dream state in an elevated emotion.

If you've had a particularly rough day and simply cannot think of a single thing to be grateful for, write something like, "I'm deeply grateful for this day to be done and I look forward to the promise of a better day tomorrow." I promise, this *will* get easier each day.

As you are journaling, you may find you get an emotional release that helps you work through your "stuff." Make notes on how you felt during the day. Recording your emotions is more powerful than recording your thoughts. Force yourself to find one good thing in everything that has occurred.

If you get a flash of inspiration or a message from the angels, make note of it. After a few days, you will find more things for which to be grateful. You may also start to become clearer about some the sources of your negative world view. It may be toxic relationships, work environment, or upbringing. You may have adopted or inherited a victim mentality. You will also become clearer about what you are trying to achieve with your spiritual awakening.

With this newfound clarity, you will be more capable of cutting through toxicity from others, or even from yourself. It's likely a habit. You might not have ever thought of negative speaking and thinking patterns as problematic. If the source if primarily internal, that's good news! You have the power to make new choices and revamp your thinking and your worldview. If it's primarily your surroundings, that's a bit tougher. You may need to make some hard choices about relationships and work environments that are toxic. That will come. But first make the commitment to keep a gratitude journal for twenty-one days.

All this work will be raising your frequencies and preparing you for more angelic communication. As you declutter the dark closets of your past, you will be able to make decisions about what to keep, what to get rid of, and how to reorganize things so they are more useful to you in the future. It seems scary and unmanageable in the beginning but becomes easier as you go. And the end result will allow you more room in your life for happiness and joy.

Calling In Your Angels

Now that you know how to create your sacred space and how to quiet your mind, you are ready to call in your angels. It's as easy as tuning into the proper radio station and enjoying the broadcast. After a while, you learn to live at a higher frequency level, and you will find the angels are around you most of the time. In the beginning, you might have to go through several steps to get to where you've prepared a space for them to come. Relax. This gets easier with practice.

Follow the instructions on creating your sacred space and start your meditation. Once you've quieted your mind, respectfully call on the angel with whom you wish to communicate.

I work primarily with the archangels. Here is a very brief summary of the angels I work with and what you might expect from them. I invite you to conduct your own research to expand your knowledge of the angelic realm. There are volumes of information online and at the libraries. This information was inspired by the work of Master Nona.

Ariel means "altar" or "lion of God" in Hebrew. Other spellings include Ari'el, Arael, and Ariael. Ariel is known as the angel of nature and is often associated with the color purple and the direction of east. (S)he is the angel of light in the Prayer of Protection: "The Light of God

191

surrounds us." Ask Archangel Ariel for help in being able to see clearly and accurately. Look to Ariel for help in balance and anything to do with nature.

Raphael is known as the angel of healing and is often surrounded by the color of green and associated with the direction of west. His name means "healer, doctor, surgeon" in Hebrew. He is also associated with the angel of love in the Prayer of Protection: "The Love of God enfolds us." Call on Archangel Raphael for healing at all levels.

Michael is known as the one "who is as God," or "looks like God." His color is usually orange, and his direction is south. He's known as the defender of light and goodness and the protector of the weak. In the Prayer of Protection, he is "the Power of God [that] protects us."

Gabriel, or "Governor of Light," is known as the Presence of God in the protection prayer. "The Presence of God watches over us." He brings God's messages and prophecies. He can guide you to fulfill your hopes and dreams, deal with your karmic issues, and progress on the path toward harmony with all.

Uriel is known as the angel of wisdom and truth. He will shine the light of God's wisdom into your life. He can help if you are working through old, false beliefs that are limiting your spiritual growth.

Metatron works with sacred geometry and is thought to be one of the only two angels that actually started out as a human on earth before becoming an angel. The other angel is Sandalphon. Archangel Metatron comes in a green and purple energy, and he helps with clearing out negative beliefs, fears, and just clearing your energy in general. When he's showed up in my meditations, I found his energy and presence was huge, both in intensity and size.

Hosting the Archangels in Your Home

There's a very cool tradition of hosting the archangels in your home. It was inspired by a continuation of a "pay it forward" project started in 2010 by a German New York–based medium named Irmi. It is said she received divine inspiration after watching the movie *Pay It Forward*.

By hosting the archangels, she asserts you are assisting them to serve humanity and Mother Earth in more direct ways. I've hosted them four times and always find it profound. I'll briefly describe the process and provide a link if you would like to host them yourself. The archangels you would host are Michael, Gabriel, Raphael, Uriel, Metatron, and Ariel.

Here are the instructions from Bellésprit blog.[4]

Preparation Ritual: You will welcome and host the Archangels for 5 days after having prepared a little altar with:

- A white flower.

---

[4] https://www.bellesprit.com/hosting-the-archangels-in-your-home/

- A candle that will stay on the entire time they are with you. It needs to be on shortly before they arrive to show them where they are being called. An electronic flame candle is fine. If you use a regular candle it can be blown out when you go out. It is to be left burning whenever you are in your home and while you sleep in a safe container.

- Put in an envelope a letter with three wishes: one for Mother Earth, one for your family, one for you. Formulate the wishes in a clear and concise way. Not too many details. Summarize as best you can. Each member of the household should write their own wishes down in and place in the envelope.

- On the sealed envelope, you will put an apple (one for each participant) that will be eaten after they leave. Lay the envelope near your candle and white flower. The house should be clean and tidy much like you would do if you were about to receive guests.

Welcoming the Five Archangels: When they arrive in front of your home at 10:30 p.m. you are to open the front door and read this greeting:

"Hello and welcome Archangels to my home. You were sent to me from _____. (Insert your name of who sent the angels to you.) I am incredibly grateful to each of you for purifying and bringing peace to this place and to the beings that live in it. I am grateful to you for bringing harmony, joy and serenity to all of us. I am grateful to you for fulfilling my wishes."

From that moment on, the Archangels make things happen. It is recommended to regard the five days as a special time to give room for the vibration of higher energies to realign many things. For some, this may mean you want to meditate and to ask questions or you may only be able to find a quiet moment in your busy day, but remember, there is no limitation, TRUST. You can also ask them to go with you as you go through your day. Start to prepare the list of the names and addresses of the three or more people who you will ask the Archangels to visit next after you, along with a letter of instructions. The number three is a recommendation only. If you have trouble finding someone to pass them on to, let the person who sent them to you know, so they can help keep the energy moving to new people.

At the end of the 5th day:

When it is almost time for them to leave (just before 10:30 p.m.), write the names of each person who has asked to host the archangels next on a piece of paper, and set it near your candle for a few minutes to soak up the light. When it feels right, walk outside with your candle, the piece of paper and express your gratitude to the archangels for all they have brought you. Light the paper on fire in a safe way with the candle. This will pass their names into the ethers and to the archangels along with the addresses where the angels will be going next after five days of rest. Wish them a good trip and give more thanks and good wishes, as they journey on to spread their hope, light and love to others who will be hosting them.

Once they leave:
• Burn the envelope with your wishes in it. This frees up the energy and allows the wishes to manifest. Take the ashes and drop them in a stream of water (not stagnant water). If you live in a cold country, the kitchen sink is acceptable as the water will be recycled to Mother Earth or out into the wind. Once again, express your gratitude.
• Eat the apple. It will contain lots of good nutrients and more for you.
• Place the flower outside directly on Mother Earth so that it recycles in a natural way.
• Send this ritual to the people who will host them next if you haven't already. (Update these dates and names for your own letter to your friends.)

In the meantime, you will need to find the suggested three people or more for hosting the archangels.

To review, after leaving each home, the angels will rest for five days before the start of the next visit with your friend.

It has been found that people either really want to do this or they don't or can't. The people who have done it before always want to do it again. Remember this is not a chain letter. It is closer to a pass it on message.

YOU, YOUR HOME, EVERYONE AND EVERYTHING IN YOUR HOME WILL BE BLESSED BY THE ANGELS DURING THE TIME OF THEIR VISIT WITH YOU. IT HELPS OUR WORLD TO ANCHOR MORE LIGHT, PEACE AND LOVE INTO YOUR DWELLING.

You can invite them to go with you as you go about your five days.

Having them here will help you experience peace and tranquility. They will assist you in calmly carrying out your tasks and keeping your space sacred, peaceful and loving.

Thank you for being interested in hosting the Archangels.

If you would like to be part of this project, simply start five days after viewing this article. You can list your name and details in the comments below if seeking for others to pass the angels on to. Don't forget to pay it forward!

For now, it helps to learn a little more about what the angels might bring to you. Here is some information on the vibration or energies of each of these Great Rays of

Creation and Reality, also known as Archangels:

Gabriel—"My task is to guide you to fulfill your hopes and dreams, deal with your karmic issues and progress on the path towards harmony with all. This requires a balance between the active side of you and the passive side of you. I am the spiritual awakener who visits you in your dreams, bringing you fresh hope, intuition and new aspirations."

Raphael—"I come on a pure spiral that flows from Father Sun to manifest all life on Mother Earth. It is the glorious energy ray whose nurturing warmth brings you joy of living, banishes darkness and enlightens your life and future. I aid you in making decisions, using logic and analytical skills, and taking action accordingly."

Michael—"As lord of light and ruler of Mercury, my primary gift to you is communication and truth. I strengthen and protect you. My Light dispels all darkness and falsehood from your life. My golden sword lights your way to truth, wisdom and freedom."

Uriel—"Many and mysterious are the ways I manifest on Mother Earth. I bring fire and alchemy through the cleansing fires of purification. All old programming can be burnt away and all blocks within rendered down to ash. My energy empowers you, securing the foundation on which to build your new self.

Collectively, my alchemy flames bring infinite possibility."

Metatron—"I am the guardian of the Tree of Life. Both the base and the summit are your points of connection to the Creator and All Life. I guide you toward the sanctuary of the pure white dove of peace. Let your spirituality gradually become supremely important, for as you reach the crown, you grasp the secret wisdom of All. My twin angel, Shekinah helps you to secure your foundation in the earthly kingdom. As you reconnect with All Life through sacred geometry, you will send and receive Love and Light, magnifying it within your heart for the benefit of All Life."

Ariel—"I help those who call upon me to recognize the sacred spark within Nature and all living things and beings. As an angel associated with metaphysics and manifestation, I can help you understand how to use the Law of Attraction, not simply as a tool to use for personal gain but for the advancement of all life. Look to me if you wish to awaken to a collective level of consciousness and manifestation, or for how to manifest peace, love and balance within your greater world. For, I can teach those who call upon me how to more purposefully create a bridge between Heaven and Earth; Spirit and Matter; Father God and Mother Nature; Yin and Yang. I often work as a companion angel to Archangel Raphael; the Archangel governing Healing."

On the last day of their visit at your home, give the Archangels the names and addresses of the people you find who want to host them next. You will need to send these people the information and simple ritual below and specify to them the date of arrival and departure of the Archangels from their home. The time (10:30 p.m.) stays the same, no matter the time difference. It is always the local time. The day is 24 hours long. The Archangels' visit is always five days, and then they rst for five days before coming back for another five day visit with a new host. The five-day process of rest/visit/rest/visit continues as people pass it on.

Note: If you don't have anyone to invite you, consider this article an invitation or ask the Universe for an invitation. You host the angels consecutively or as many times as you wish. What is most important is your intention and the purpose is to have a time of meditation, reflection and connection where you are less disturbed by daily life and its demands so you can focus on a connection to something higher. If you have no one to pass your angels along to, just ask they visit those who need them.

Reprinted with permission.

In Closing

Everyone and anyone can and should call on their guardian angels and archangels whenever they can. They are there for you. They want to help you. They will respond to your requests. But they must be invoked. What are you waiting for? Let this be your invitation to start or continue your spiritual journey. I promise you it will be amazing. It will also rock your world.

I can tell you that this work has brought me a calm I have never experienced. In making the connections to the angels, feeling their love, and hearing their guidance, I am no longer confused. If I have a choice as to who to believe regarding the true nature of my existence and the Universe, I'll take the angels' perspective on that subject any day over my human counterparts.

Closing Message from Archangel Raphael

This was channeled in 2020 early in the pandemic, and everyone was feeling hopeless about their job loss and having to be isolated.

The problem isn't with feeling good about your work or your contribution to society. The problem isn't in a sudden abrupt loss. The issue is that you were looking outside of yourself to define who you are.

And boy, don't we all do that. In other words, looking outside of yourself for who you are is risky business at best and dangerous at its core.

Don't allow outside circumstances to define you. It ignores the obvious, that you are identifying with your physical self, not your spiritual self. The reason that it can hurt so much and be so destructive is because it is not true. You are not your career. You are not your work. You are not your job. You are a spiritual being, having a physical experience.

When you get that fundamental reality, then the bumps and the detours become just that. Bumps and detours to go around, not dead ends. Your spiritual self cannot be denied its existence. Unfold and blossom in the direction of the light, the sun, and you will thrive. In your time of reflection, hear the truth. You are a spiritual being, having a physical experience. You are an expression of God. When you forget that is when you get bogged down in this amazing, wonderful, dangerous, fabulous, physical expression.

Soar above, see your truth. See your truth. Ask the angels for help. We do want to assist you. We want to help you see the light, the truth, God's divine plan for your life. We want to help you lift above your earthly burdens. Give them to us. Please don't ask for them back.

I love it when they have a sense of humor.

We want to provide spiritual comfort and a deep [and they had me underline that several times], *deep knowing you are never alone.* [And when they told me that I started getting emotional.] *A warm, divine hug anytime you need it. These are the things that we want to help you with.*

We want to help you clarify your divine nature and assist you in following God's divine plan for your life. Remember, God designed you to be strong and resilient. Trust that truth. This, too, shall pass. We are with you, and we love you. —Archangel Raphael

Bibliography

Bostrom, Nick. "Are You Living in a Computer Simulation?" *Philosophical Quarterly* 53, no. 211 (2003): 243-255. www.simulation-argument.com.

Yvonne Perry, "What Is Light Language?," We Are 1 in Spirit (website), accessed October 1, 2020, https://weare1inspirit.com/what-is-light-language.

Dr. Alberto Villoldo, What Is A Despacho?, "The Four Winds (website), accessed October 1, 2020, https://thefourwinds.com/blog/shamanism/what-is-a-despacho/

Online Resources
You will find my channeled angel messages on
my YouTube Channel,
YouTube.com/NiceRockShop

For my website and contact information:
NiceRockShop.com
NiceRockShop@gmail.com
TheBalancedEmpath.com
SusanKEdwards.com

Made in United States
Troutdale, OR
05/20/2025

31521829R00132